When Momma Speaks

Dear Lotette,

What a blessing &
delight you have been
over the years. May these
words speak divine favor
and sweet peace for
your path! Love you
dearly!

[signature]

3/8/18

When Momma Speaks

The Bible and Motherhood
from a Womanist Perspective

Stephanie Buckhanon
Crowder

WESTMINSTER
JOHN KNOX PRESS
LOUISVILLE · KENTUCKY

© 2016 Stephanie Buckhanon Crowder

First edition
Published by Westminster John Knox Press
Louisville, Kentucky

16 17 18 19 20 21 22 23 24 25—10 9 8 7 6 5 4 3 2 1

Scripture quotations from the New Revised Standard Version of the Bible are copyright © 1989 by the Division of Christian Education of the National Council of the Churches of Christ in the U.S.A. and are used by permission.

Scripture taken from *The Message.* Copyright © 1993, 1994, 1995, 1996. Used by permission of NavPress Publishing Group.

Book design by Drew Stevens
Cover design by Allison Taylor
Cover art: Flower Mother with Child, Tamara Adams. Used by permission.

Library of Congress Cataloging-in-Publication Data
Names: Crowder, Stephanie R. Buckhanon, 1969- author.
Title: When momma speaks : the Bible and motherhood from a womanist perspective / Stephanie Buckhanon Crowder.
Description: Nth edition. | Louisville, Ky : Westminster John Knox Press, [2016] | Includes bibliographical references and index.
Identifiers: LCCN 2016006692 (print) | LCCN 2016015073 (ebook) | ISBN 9780664239251 (alk. paper) | ISBN 9781611646788 (e-book)
Subjects: LCSH: Mothers in the Bible. | Bible and feminism. | Bible--Feminist criticism. | African American women--Religious life.
Classification: LCC BS579.M65 C76 2016 (print) | LCC BS579.M65 (ebook) | DDC 220.6082--dc23
LC record available at http://lccn.loc.gov/2016006692

♾ The paper used in this publication meets the minimum requirements of the American National Standard for Information Sciences—Permanence of Paper for Printed Library Materials, ANSI Z39.48-1992.

Most Westminster John Knox Press books are available at special quantity discounts when purchased in bulk by corporations, organizations, and special-interest groups. For more information, please e-mail SpecialSales@wjkbooks.com.

In memory of
my grandmother Maggie Florence Edwards Rowland
and
my mother, JoAnn Givand, whose suicide yet shapes my life

Contents

Acknowledgments   ix

Introduction   xi

Part One: Setting the Stage

1. Being an African American Mother   3

2. Womanist Maternal Thought   17

3. Womanist Biblical Interpretation   28

Part Two: Revealing the Characters

4. Hagar: A Homeless Mother (Genesis 16 and 21:8–21)   41

5. Rizpah: A Childless Mother (2 Samuel 21:1–14)   52

6. Bathsheba: A Fearless Mother (1 Kings 1:11–31)   63

7. Mary: A Favor(less) Mother (Luke 1:26–38)   73

8. The Canaanite Woman: A Relentless Mother
   (Matthew 15:21–28)   84

9. Zebedee's Wife: A Shameless Mother (Matthew 20:20–28)   92

Part Three: Final Act

10. Where Do We Go from Here?   105

Selected Bibliography   111

Index   119

Acknowledgments

I am grateful to you for purchasing this book. In this day and age when there is so much available online, thank you for engaging this expression of my thoughts and ruminations. The idea for this project started over eight years ago as I found myself preaching on various women in the Bible. As a "lady preacher," I figured that I should write this book. The task became more daunting as I sought new ways of telling the old stories on Mother's Day. I cannot say I have found much joy preaching on this sacred day. Honestly, I am a little jaded. I think my mother's suicide yet leaves me in a state of dis-ease and discomfort.

However, reading the stories of biblical mothers and delivering sermons on them have removed some scales from my eyes. Additionally my own journey into motherhood has forced me to corner whatever maternal dilemmas I faced as a child with my own mother. Ironically, when I speak to my children, I often hear her voice. Life is funny that way. Until you walk in someone's shoes, you really cannot comprehend or appreciate her story. I am humbled by the many congregations that allowed me to share their pulpit as I wrestled with the biblical figures in this book.

I want to thank my editor, Bridgett Green, who is such a joy and inspiration. She often sees beyond what I see. Westminster John Knox Press has a jewel in her. I work with such a warm, hardworking group at Chicago Theological Seminary; thank you for "letting me be myself."

My sister-preachers—Rev. Joanne Robertson, Dr. Christal Williams, and Rev. Sekinah Hamblen—you keep me grounded, heretical, and laughing. To my fellow womanist biblical scholars, I am delighted our circle is growing. I am grateful for the opportunity to test some of this material on Park Manor Christian Church. You were such good students. Drs. Fernando and Elena Segovia and Dr. Sharon Watson Fluker continue to provide sound professional advice, even in this stage in my career. They are true mentors and friends indeed.

My aunts (Lois and Cathy), uncles, cousins, godmother (Arline), and friends (Melody and Regenia) call to my remembrance the seeds of North Memphis planted in my being. I dedicate this to my grand-mother Maggie Rowland, who was just "ol'-skool" amazing. I still feel her presence, and her voice resoundingly whispers in my ear. My mother, JoAnn Givand, committed suicide. She made a decision for me in the sixth grade that changed my academic trajectory! Still her pain pushes me. To "Crowder" I could apologize for kicking you off the computer all of those nights, but I really needed to finish this book. I appreciate your understanding. And to my sons: what I have written reflects in one way or another the mother you have made me to be.

Divine One, My Mother and My Father, I am humbled that you still pursue me.

Something just happens—when Momma speaks.

Introduction

I was speaking at another Women's Day celebration. I say "another" not because I had grown accustomed or tired of this type of engagement but because of sheer gratitude that another church asked me to help honor the labor, love, and spirit that is woman. After preaching, I spent time hugging and shaking hands here and there. There was indeed a rich spirit in the room. The attendees were very complimentary and expressed appreciation for my participation.

As I was about to leave, one of the program's co-chairpersons approached me. She boldly declared, "You have written a lot of material. Your bio is quite impressive." I shyly thanked her and proceeded to walk away because I thought the pause indicated the end of the conversation. She continued, "I was wondering what resource do you have for single mothers? There are a large number of mothers, especially young ones, who need some help, some guidance."

I was floored. I had traveled across the United States preaching, lecturing, and giving workshops; but it was not until this woman's comment that I realized the hole in my scholarship. From an academic stance, I had often discussed the role of social location and identity. I even scheduled classes and meetings around my identity as a mother so that, if at all possible, I would not miss one of my son's parent-teacher conferences or sports events. I had toyed with my personhood as a mother in the university's hallowed halls. I had juggled my who-ness as a mom and professor on innumerable occasions. However, I had not put the two-ness of motherhood and academician together in written form. It was not until after what I thought was "another" preaching opportunity that my scholarship had an anagnorisis, an academic aha-moment.

I needed to combine my way of thinking about the Bible and how I get meaning from it with my social identity as a mother, professor, wife, scholar, and preacher. I could no longer speak, get my check, and leave. Mothers longed for me to use my gifts in the academy and the church to help "make it plain," "make motherhood plain." Women had to have more. The metes and bounds of my vocation in the academy and in the church called for more. What better way to give this more than to write afresh, write something, write more.

Hence, I began playing with the idea of womanist maternal thought. I first noticed "womanist" while reading Alice Walker's book, *In Search of Our Mothers' Garden*.[1] Whereas she includes an extensive definition of the term, what struck me was the line "loves herself."[2] I did love who I was as a preacher, teacher, and author. I definitely loved who I was as a mother; and, thanks to a conversation with another woman, my scholarship would reflect this.

Yet this brief exchange after a local church event was not the only watershed moment in my writing and thinking. The following experience also served to redirect my publishing and what I was to share with women who balance two professions: motherhood and career.

I was sitting in a room full of mothers. At first glance the gathering was not unusual. Yet I was also in a room full of African American biblical scholars. This was our first such gathering at the Society of Biblical Literature, or SBL. This is a professional organization primarily comprising individuals who teach Old Testament (sometimes called Hebrew Bible) and New Testament biblical studies in colleges, universities, seminaries, and divinity schools. Whereas we knew of each other and had engaged one another's work in our respective courses, we had not officially gathered until that November evening in 2008 in a Boston hotel.

As we introduced ourselves and our areas of specialty, I was stunned to learn how many of us had children. Of the approximately thirty women in the room, more than half shared something about being a mother. We were not ashamed of our parental roles, but the academic arena was and still is not hospitable. "The firm is ambivalent towards family." Our fellowship in itself was novel and cause for much celebration. This was the first gathering of African American female professors of biblical studies at the SBL. The Society itself is predominately white and male. Moreover, the revelation of our duties outside the hallowed halls of academia spurred additional jubilation. In a sense of communal affirmation, we learned that we answered to more than just "Professor,"

---

1. Alice Walker, *In Search of Our Mothers' Gardens: Womanist Prose* (Orlando: Harcourt Inc., 1983).
2. Ibid., xii. Some elements of Walker's definition of "womanist" that are relevant to this work include "from womanism; a black feminist or feminist of color; acting womanish; interested in grown-up doings; appreciates and prefers women's culture, committed to survival and wholeness of entire people; loves struggle; loves Folk; loves herself."

"Dr.," or "Ms." We had heard and responded to the clarion call of "Mommy," "Mom," and, in some cases, "Grandma."

It is out of this "double consciousness"[3] that so many African American female scholars in general have had to survive. We have had to remain hush-hush about children and families. It is humorous, or not, that many of our children have academic birthdays because we planned our pregnancies or adoptions around the institutional calendar. Any number of us have children born in May or June so as not to interfere with our school's exams and/or graduation dates. Yes, we bring our families to professional meetings; however, there is still limited discussion of the intersection of family and career. It was not until 2011 that I noticed the Society of Biblical Literature offering childcare. In the same year there was at least one session on mothering.

As mother scholars or want-to-be mother scholars, we cannot overlook the "off the record" questions at job interviews about family or plans for children. Many pretenure females hear a "hint" or outright warning to wait to have children until after they have completed this matriculation process. Issues of maternity leave, timing, and class coverage are the elephant in the academic room. Therein is the use of the term "mother scholars" and not scholarly mothers.

Latina, Asian, African, and Caucasian female professionals endure the same struggles. However, I am not speaking for them or for all mothers in the African diaspora. I write from only my own social location and experiences as an African American New Testament scholar who on one day submitted a final dissertation draft and literally give birth again the very next day. Chapter 1 provides a historical overview of what it means to be a mother within an African American context. It examines the images of motherhood from various contexts: African, African American chattel slavery, "mammy" in the Reconstruction era, unsung mothers of the civil rights movement, godmother/play mothers, "baby mama" drama, teen mothers, stay-at-home mothers, the Mocha Moms network, pastor/preacher mothers, and mothering in politics.

There has been a close-knit relationship and perhaps convergence of my identity as academic and mother since I first entered the academy over twenty years ago. It is out of this ontology that I have come to wrestle with the idea of womanist maternal thinking.[4] Although

3. W. E. B. DuBois, *The Souls of Black Folk* (Rockville, MD: Arc Manor Publishing, 2008), 12. Originally published in 1903.

4. Stephanie Buckhanon Crowder, "Biblical/African American Mother Working/Wrecking," *Semeia Studies* 61 (November 2009):157–67.

my interest in African American women scholars and motherhood resurfaced in 2008, I first coined the phrase "womanist maternal thinking" in 2006 when presenting at the Southeastern Conference on the Study of Religion (SECSOR) meeting. Here I discussed the meaning of the Canaanite mother's work as advocacy and a representation of African American mothers' labor.

I will pursue womanist maternal thinking in chapter 2, where I expound on this new area of study: that is, womanist maternal hermeneutics. By defining "womanism" as a field of study that seeks to interpret simultaneously African American women's and the African American community's experience in the context of theology or God-talk and "motherhood" as advocacy and activity that women initiate to bring wholeness and health to children, the chapter shows how this new field of study is different from feminist maternal theology and why this approach fills a void in women's studies. This chapter pays particular attention to the relevance of womanist maternal thinking for African American mothers in the United States.

Under the rubric of womanist biblical hermeneutics, chapter 3 focuses on the ways in which African American women tend to read and interpret biblical texts in light of their own experiences. Additionally this chapter outlines the metes and bounds of womanist biblical studies as an approach rooted in the ways that the bible informs African American women's lives and their understanding of faith. The chapter explains how this model of interpretation encompasses the manner in which African American women's experiences affect their reading of the Bible.

Womanist biblical interpretation as the theoretical framework for chapters 4 through 8 becomes the exegetical lens to sample biblical mothers from the Hebrew Bible and New Testament. Chapter 4 examines the surrogacy of Hagar. She is a homeless, displaced mother whose role as a substitute mother backfires. Hagar's story serves as the impetus for addressing women and children living in shelters while expounding on modern-day surrogacy.

Chapter 5 recounts the story of Rizpah. She does not relinquish her motherly duties even after her children die: she continues to guard their bodies from further harm. Furthermore, she renders the same degree of attention to another mother's children. This chapter also addresses the current context of mothers who have lost children to violence, war, early death, and "dead" situations of children on drugs, in prison, in gangs, or just living dangerously.

Chapter 6 examines Bathsheba as a fearless mother. Despite her "past" with David, she confronts him on his deathbed regarding his promise to make Solomon the next king. Bathsheba is a woman who boldly plays a man's game. This chapter expounds on African American mothers trying to survive in a "man's" corporate world.

I chose the mothers from the Hebrew Bible/Old Testament because they are women who were subjects of sermons I preached over the years. There stories had not been told from this interpretive perspective. Honestly, I have not heard any sermon on Rizpah, and there was little research on her. The novelty and the fact that much of this approach was unchartered territory appealed to me.

Chapter 7 presents a divergent view of Mary the mother of Jesus. An angel says God favors Mary, but Mary initially rejects this favor and is therefore favorless. She is uncomfortable with God's promise and insecure in the future. This chapter discusses Mary as a teen and leads into an exploration of the state of teenage mothers and stigmas surrounding them. It also seeks to delineate the ideas that mothers are sometimes uncertain about what to do, and that is OK; motherhood can be clouded with personal insecurity, social stigma, and financial instability.

The Canaanite mother is the subject of chapter 8. She is relentless in that she does not stop seeking Jesus despite his and the disciples' attempts to send her away. She endures harsh language and circumstances for the sake of her child's healing. This chapter will include discussion of women who go to extreme lengths to advocate for children, women whom society labels as "other" due to race, and women who engage institutional powers for the good of the children.

The image of one negotiating a place of honor for her sons describes the mother of James and John in chapter 9. She makes a bold request filled with effrontery. As a mother she goes straight to Jesus and seeks places of prestige for her children. Her concern is for the social mobility of her children. This chapter explores the current context of maternal materialism and the pressure for children to succeed in cases of the mother's lack of success. It explores how mothers live vicariously through their children.

I chose these New Testament mothers because I have also preached sermons about them. Additionally, like the women from the first testament, few scholars, if any, narrate their stories with this particular sociological, political, and theological lens. Their actions and responses to Jesus or God's agent are compelling and out of the box.

Chapter 10 concludes the book by reviewing main ideas and offering maternal tentacles for the future. There are many biblical mothers not addressed in this book. Also as situations regarding current-day mothers are constantly changing, the final chapter offers some preliminary points of departure for future research.

Study questions are included in each chapter to facilitate both personal and communal reflection and, yes, action.

Needless to say, this book has been a long time coming. It is the culmination of years of wrestling with aspects of my identity and trying to find some way to teach, write, and preach myself through the dissonance. This project is also meant to be communal. As previously stated, almost half the biblical scholars laughing, talking, and, yes, crying on that cold evening in Boston were mothers. So many since that time have become mothers. I want this book to be a resource so that my sisters in the academy will not suffer in silence or become voiceless victims. The academy does not have the right to dictate what we do with our bodies inside or outside of the academy.

As the question that prompted these ruminations emanated from a church setting, I want this book to ultimately be a guide, handbook, how-to manual, a reflection resource for women who will never step foot in a seminary or divinity school or who may not have gone to college. I want to be able to point women and men to a work that examines African American motherhood from a biblical perspective. This work is meant to be practical in nature and go beyond thought and meditation. Yes, one must think and analyze one's actions in order to change. Nonetheless, as a tool of praxis, the purpose of this book is to give African American mother steps, tidbits to developing and enriching the ministry that is called "Mom," "Momma," or "Ma-Dear."

I seek to foster change of behavior and habits within African American women who as mothers, by any definition, have the privilege of nurturing the next generation of girls and boys. For a mother of any racial or ethnic background, this work seeks to shed light on mothers in the Bible whose stories in some way resonate with their lives. As mothers there are certain expectations and demands society places on us. This role sometimes poses challenges to our additional professional obligations. Yet, as mommas, we dare not put anything or anyone before our children. We dare to risk it all for another hug, another kiss, or attendance at baby boy's or baby girl's events. We take extreme strides to salvage who we are as "momma."

Whether you read it entirely from beginning to end, study it with a small group, or select specific chapters that meet you where you are, this book seeks to help you traverse this journey called motherhood. Sometimes the road is rocky and replete with lions and tigers and bears. There are moments when there is a clear, maternal path. Whoever you are, wherever you are in life, it is my design that what is written in these pages will offer helpful hints and lessons learned as we mothers discover and embrace the strength that oft lies dormant. Ours is a powerful voice even in the stillest moments. It is a voice that will not give way to hatred or injustice. In a mother's tongue is a child's future, a community's rallying cry. Recall this book project came to being after I was speaking to another woman following a preaching engagement. The sacred, self, and society lend an ear and stir into action—when Momma speaks!

PART ONE
Setting the Stage

1

Being an African American Mother

We need mothers who are capable of being character builders, patient, loving, strong and true, whose homes will be uplifting power in the race. This is one of the greatest needs of the hour.
—Frances Ellen Watkins Harper, "Enlightened Motherhood," 1892

This is not your mother's idea of motherhood. Society no longer views the maternal through the eyes of Florida Evans from *Good Times*, Carole Brady from *The Brady Bunch*, or Mrs. Cleaver from *Leave It to Beaver*.[1] Hollywood has made being a mommy as hot as haute couture. Images of Halle Berry, Beyoncé, Angela Bassett, Tyra Banks, and even rapper Lil' Kim seek to add glitz and glamor to the maternal world. Mega-producer and self-proclaimed titan, Shonda Rhimes has added to the motherhood conversation in her recent book and TED Talk. She maintains saying "yes" to play makes for better work.[2] Mothers throughout the United States watched the first African American First Lady, Michelle Obama. From the time she first appeared on the campaign trail in 2007 and throughout the Obama family's White House days, women wanted to know how this Mom-in-Chief was nurturing her daughters, Sasha and Malia. Surely she would be the ultimate, übermom. Yes, the images of the maternal have shifted from aprons and kitchens to designer bags and boardrooms. Mommies rock!

Yet whereas these are modern-day presentations of motherhood, time will not forget the plethora of nameless so-called mammies and

1. *Good Times, The Brady Bunch* and *Leave It to Beaver* were sitcoms during the 1970s. *Good Times* featured a poor black family living in Chicago whereas *The Brady Bunch* and *Leave It to Beaver* centered around middle-class white families living in the suburbs. In all three shows, the mother was a stay-at-home domestic figure primarily responsible for running the household.
2. Shonda Rhimes, "My Year of Saying Yes to Everything," TED Talk, https://www.ted.com/talks/shonda_rhimes_my_year_of_saying_yes_to_everything?language=en.

matriarchs. There are those who during slavery and the Reconstruction nursed not only their children, but "massah's" children as well. These were hardworking, burden-bearing, heavy-load carrying foremothers who from sunup to sundown worked in the fields only to go home and provide for their own sons and daughters. It was only after they took care of somebody's child that they could focus on being mother to their own. The field or the domestic job called them first.

At the cusp of the twentieth century, society stood in need of the work only a mother could do. The quote from Frances Ellen Watkins Harper alludes to this. The nurturing, maternal presence of a woman was the order of the day then. There is still a clarion call for such labor now. If indeed the work of mothers is that of character building, it is also the construction of stately, human edifices who will change the landscape of the environment.

Children spend hours upon hours at school and days and weeks at camp. In these places they encounter peers whose ways of thinking, doing, and believing are different from their own. Such distinctions are primarily due to different parents teaching their children in different ways at different times. So much of this teaching comes from a maternal figure. Thus there comes to the forefront the need for mothers in the home where children can learn sociological and spiritual values that will undergird them for life. Training in the home must combat what goes on outside of its environs. Along with primarily overseeing the domestic responsibilities of the house, mothers tend to be the principle teachers and nurturers.

The operative words are "primarily" and "tend." It is no doubt that many children do not live in a two-parent household. Quite a few children reside with only a father and no maternal figure. Almost two million men are single fathers, and 16 percent of custodial single parents are men.[3] In addition there are conditions in households where the mother is the breadwinner and the onus of dishes, bills, and homework lies with the dad. An estimated 195,000 men are stay-at-home dads who have remained out of the labor force for at least a year so that they can care for the family while their wives work outside the home.[4] Thus there is no one-size-fits-all approach to what it means to be a mother, especially in an African American context. In many ways there is no norm. To each household its "motherly" own.

3. "Dad Stats," U.S. Department of Health and Human Services, https://www.fatherhood.gov/content/dad-stats.
4. Ibid.

In addition, biological mothering does not mean that a woman is adept at motherhood. There is no magical, maternal gene that gets turned on because a woman gives birth or adopts a child. Motherhood is a process. It is a journey. It may or may not begin with desire, but a part of becoming a mother is perchance growing into this state of being.

There, I said it. This idea of motherhood is not monolithic. It is not universal. There are some "ifs," "ands," or "buts" that make the definition and its task nebulous at best. Nonetheless, what this research tries to do is show that there are some common ideas and tenets about maternal existence. There are aspects of motherhood that are indeed universal and warrant further investigation.

This labor of "character building," as Harper calls it, has not always been easy for women of African descent. Whereas the independence in some African countries allowed mothers to rule, love, and nurture at will, the crisis of the Middle Passage and subsequent slave trade made this task arduous and painful at best.

Understanding motherhood within an African American context lends to some examination of its origin in West African cultures. Because Africans that were brought to America primarily came from West Africa, viewing maternity through this lens is a beginning. Scholars differ on whether West African ideas on motherhood were reconstituted in America or left behind altogether. Frazier argues that due to slavery, "there was no social organization to sustain whatever conceptions of life the Negro might have retained of his African heritage."[5] On the contrary, Herskovits maintains that there is the "presence of Africanisms in black family life and in various other aspects of black culture."[6] While they differ about origin, both arguments assert that the focus on consanguinity versus conjugality as approaches to family are at the core of the African versus Western family foundation. Consanguinity is the focus on bloodties that connect the family whereas a conjugality is based on legal procedures that bring people together as family i.e. marriage. African family structures hold to the idea of bloodlines as a means of creating community and commonality counter to Western ideas that tend to value marriage as a means of unifying people.

The arguments of Herskovits and Frazier have limits as well as

5. Niara Sudarkasa, "Roots of the African American Family: Observations on the Frazier-Herskovits Debate," in *The Strength of Our Mothers: African and African American Women and Families* (Trenton: Africa Word, 1996), 81.
6. Ibid.

advantages. Yet neither discounts the role of mother in elements of West African culture and its presence in America. In some West African countries, matrilineality serves as a means for determining the allocation of land, titles, and other properties among their mothers. In such societies, a woman's children belong to the lineage of the mother. Children of the same mother belong to the same matrilineage regardless of paternity.[7] Relationships are linked through the descent of the mother-line. It is the consanguineal connection or bloodline that forms the core of the community's relationship and serves as the root of the extended family. The matrilineal ties include not only living family members but also the ancestors of the mother.

Even in cases of a patrilineal structure where ancestry is rooted in the father, the mothers still have a significant role that in some cases can transcend the role of their husbands. This is primarily due to family lineage rooted in the wives. They help to tie one family to another family, thus extending the bonds of not only one family but two. If a particular community practices polygamy, then there are even more connectors among various family groups. Another distinction between patrilineal and matrilineal frameworks is that the males in matrilineal societies cannot occupy the roles that are strictly analogous to those of females in patrilineal societies. If for no other reason, it is the women in both instances who bear the children.[8]

Although not the norm in West African cultures, matrilineality in this context provides a means for scrutinizing the strong female presence in chattel slavery. While acknowledging West African tribes organized around matrilineal culture, Sudarkasa presents a different view on African American households during slavery. She maintains that "Even though these female-headed houses were not African in origin, an understanding of the importance of consanguinity in African kinship helps to explain why they persisted among black Americans as an alternative form of household organization."[9] Perchance it is that African motherhood in America was and is a recontextualized survival tactic of women, particularly mothers, who had to adjust to oppressed status as chattel slaves.

7. Ibid., 92.
8. Ibid., 97.
9. Ibid., 85.

FROM MATRILINEAL TO MAMMY

A change in environment produced a redefinition of communal structure and operation. Whereas mother as the center of family life and well-being in a West African context was something of value, this practice quickly gave way to an idea of woman as commodity and mother as supplier of the slave labor. The brutal conditions of slavery provided little room for the affective sentiment rooted in maternity. Because women's bodies were sources of capitalistic exploitation, motherhood until the 1860s was a means to finance plantation labor. Sex at the pleasure of the slave master not only soothed his egregious desires but also provided the seed to tend to his fields. Ironically, sex under such circumstances made African women on American ground more asexualized. Biologically women were mothers as they gave birth, but there was no respect for the "maternal" gift they could offer their children. Women as mothers were breeders. Children of the mothers mere field hands in the making.

Slavery limited African American women's marriage opportunities, citizenship, and humanity. There was little to no social context for issues of privatized motherhood. Children came through the loins of their mothers but did not belong to them. Slavery as a social and political milieu harnessed African American women's sexuality and fertility.[10] By redefining African American women as nonsexual beings and subsequently nullifying the humanity of children produced from sexual encounters with them, slavery uprooted what had been some West African ideas of the mother as the central force in tribe or nation building. Since the worth of women rested not in their maternal duties but in the fiscal possibilities, plantation life served to destroy communal mothering practices and accountability. By forcing women to focus on surviving rape while trying, without much success, to keep and to nurture their children, slavery took motherhood from being a social staple of the African community and made it a reflection of individualism at the hands of monetary gain.

Nonetheless the image of "mammy" as the intersection of race, gender, sexuality, and class emanated from the recontextualization of motherhood from a West African to enslaved American environment. The notion of a happy female slave who delighted in childbearing and child-rearing was the social and political product of an asexualized

10. Patricia Hill Collins, *Black Feminist Thought: Knowledge, Consciousness, and the Politics of Empowerment* (New York: Routledge, 2000), 50.

African woman on American soil. Conversely, mammy became a type of mother figure in a context where the responsibilities of mother were inconsequential. Yes, biologically enslaved women carried the label of "mother"; however, the familial duties were secondary to their duties as producers of field hands. She had no time to love her daughters or sons, and she did not need to be loved.[11]

The lack of attention women on plantations were to give their own children became the foundation for the development of the iconic mammy figure. This public face represented to whites what it meant to be a good female slave. Mammy as a happy, dark-skinned, heavy, and healthy-looking figure became the epitome of the mother who took care of the master's seed. There was no association with nurturing her own children. Her delight was in caring for the owner's house and all who dwelled in it. Mammy was the surrogate mother in African American face and was to be the model for other women of African descent.[12]

These views of mammy were not general. To African Americans she smiled but was cunning and prone to poison the masters. Whites for the most part perceived her as the bubbly servant aiming to please her owners.[13] Yet in both frameworks, mammy was still not a sexual being. Her social roles superseded her physical appeal. W. E. B. DuBois further applied a christological metaphor in describing her. He maintained: "Above all looms the figure of the Black Mammy, one of the most pitiful of the world's Christs."[14] Mammy epitomized the mind versus body, culture versus nature, dichotomy that would distinguish her from other African American enslaved women. While on the same continuum as a more youthful, light-skinned childbearing slave, mammy became the fulfillment of what a loyal, oppressed woman should be: the blissful, asexual mother to children not her own.

Post slavery the association of mammy with master's house provided impetus for the economic exploitation of freed African American women. Although no longer on plantations, women of African heritage from the 1860s to the 1960s were still the face of domestic workers in white homes. In the 1920s alone, four-fifths of African American female wage earners not in agriculture were maids, cooks, or washerwomen. From 1890 to 1920, 90 percent of clerical and professional

11. Patricia Dixon, *African American Relationships, Marriages, and Families: An Introduction* (New York: Routledge, 2007), 71.
12. Ibid., 73.
13. Ibid.
14. W. E. B. DuBois, *The Gift of Black Folk: Negroes in the Making of America* (New York: Square One Publishers, 2009), 159.

positions went to white women.[15] African American women fit in one category, that of the house servant. They were "the help" who spent their days tending to the needs of others, sometimes incessantly at the expense of their own maternal duties.

Akin to traditional mammy, the modern-day mammy in the form of Tyler Perry's "Madea," Martin Lawrence's "Big Momma," and even Rickey Smiley's "Sister Bernice" are large, manly, primarily asexual beings. They are the caregivers who show little if no interest in their appearance. Their principal concern is ensuring the needs of those who "lord it over them" are met.

These current mammy images may be visible in the ways African American women in the corporate world find themselves "cleaning" up administrative and fiduciary mess. There are innumerable occasions in which African American women find themselves the head of a business only to realize that the house is not in order. The need to smile, grin, and put on a happy face can be the pain of educated women now in charge of the master's messy, executive house.

Women of African descent came from a familial tradition where mother-centered authority was the core of tribal life. Yet slavery sought to uproot this matrilineal focus by shifting maternal roles to that of merely breeding. This emphasis on "production" laid the groundwork for viewing enslaved women as biological machines and helped to spur the caricature of the mammy figure as an asexualized, disengaged maternal figure. She neglected her own for the sake of the white other. The relegation of women to the "big house" soon stapled freed African American women to the role of domestic ad infinitum. Mammy developed into a more overbearing image of African American motherhood, the aggressive matriarch.

OF MATRIARCHS AND OTHER MOTHERS

Dixon declares that what mammy was to white homes, the matriarch figure was to African American homes. However, while mammy was the docile domestic, the matriarch was nothing short of domineering, castrating, and wielding.[16] If mammy was dependent, then the

15. Sara Kugler, "What Does Women's Liberation Look Like?" http://www.msnbc.com/msnbc/day-9what-does-womens-liberation-look.
16. Dixon, *African American Relationships, Marriages, and Families*, 71.

matriarch was the essence of too much independence. The African American matriarch represented a failed mammy, negative stigma.[17] The Moynihan Report of 1965 rubber stamps this view, declaring that the Negro community has been forced into a matriarchal structure which, because it is to out of line with the rest of the American society, seriously retards the progress of the group as a whole.[18]

This "matriarchal structure" played out in several scenarios. It included families where the primary breadwinner was the mother even if the father was present and working. In some cases the father lived in the home but did not work. Some matriarchal family units centered around a single mother who was the sole economic and authority figure in the house. Moynihan's pejorative and skewed view presents the Negro matriarchal family in the 1960s as a problem and source of economic depravity. His sociological analysis was not the overarching perspective. It all depended on who was and who is telling the black woman's story.

Researchers like Patricia Hill Collins confirm that before the 1960s the black community had a higher percentage of families with single mothers at the helm. Yet she maintains that this structure was in no way connected to poverty or issues related to welfare dependence. It was not until feminist protests and black political activism did the equation of single mothers with being poor come into the public square. If anything, black matriarchs in whatever familial context were strong women learning to survive under harsh conditions.[19] Ironically the percentage of such families was just 22 percent compared to 8 percent or so margin in white families.[20] The numbers would increase over the decades as more African American men faced income and economic disparities, thus compelling African American women to join the labor force.

Thus the emergence of the African American matriarch as the so-called overworked, bad mother who neglected her children was due primarily to African American men's limited access to economic opportunities. Capitalistic and government social policies created a climate of duress for African American men. African American women paid the demonizing price for doing whatever was necessary to solidify the African American family unit.

17. Collins, *Black Feminist Thought*, 75.
18. Patrick Moynihan, U.S. Department of Labor, "The Tangle of Pathology," http://www.dol.gov/dol/aboutdol/history/moynchapter4.htm.
19. Collins, *Black Feminist Thought*, 75.
20. Ibid.

Sociologists further note that confusion over terms such as "household" and "family" is also the root of misunderstanding matriarchy. Whereas "households" consist of individuals sharing a common dwelling, a "family" might include kin living outside the household. Additionally, lack of clarity regarding matriarchal versus matrifocal family also lends to misinterpretation and misrepresentation. Matrifocal refers to mother/woman centeredness against the supposed dominance over males as implied in the term "matriarchal." Dominance is not a precondition for a matrifocal family unit.[21]

In a relationship twist, some would avow that the African American matriarch is even judged by African American men because she refuses to let others help her and has a "pull myself up by my own bootstrap" mentality.[22] Despite what may be perceived challenges to marriage and relationships with men in general, there has been little to discount the length the matriarch will go for the sake of her children. The literature of writers like Lorraine Hansberry is among the various works that redeem the prevailing negative stereotypes. In *A Raisin in the Sun*, the matriarch, Lena Younger, dares to move her African American family into an unwelcoming white neighborhood. Hansberry does not paint Mrs. Younger as a matriarch who degrades or emasculates men. Despite family challenges, she takes her plant and moves the family one step closer to a dream fulfilled. This is classic matriarchal strength and might.

One overlooked aspect of the matriarchal image is the relationship with other matriarchs or mothers who are the heads of households. Mother-to-mother dependence is another element of African American motherhood. Whereas these women work hard for the money outside of the home, they also lean on each other to share childcare responsibilities. The concept of "other mothering" is a component in the African American maternal tradition.

Women taking care of each other's children helped to establish a form of extended family. If formal childcare is not available or too costly, one mother substitutes for another. Other mothering means that the level of respect and honor a child gives to her or his biological mother is due the neighbor, cousin, aunt, or family friend taking care of the child. In the same vein, this secondary mother has the right to

21. Bette Dickerson, *African American Single Mothers: Understanding Their Lives and Families* (Thousand Oaks, CA: SAGE Publications, 1995), xiii.
22. Kimberly Foster, "The Continuance of African American Women Stereotypes," http://www.forharriet.com/2010/06/continuance-of-black-women-stereotypes.html#axzz44QCt1BX7.

discipline the "son" or "daughter" as she would her own. Such reciproc-
ity promotes a sense of communal responsibility that cross-connects
mothers and children. If a child misbehaves, it is not unusual to suffer
the wrath of both a community and a biological mother. Although this
level of motherly accountability may not be as prevalent today, in some
communities African American women still depend on each other to
pick up children before and after school, carpool to a practice or game,
provide a meal here and there, and just serve as an additional family
member and supporter.

Other mothering also manifests in conditions where grandmothers must care for a daughter's or son's children either by choice or by
default. Grandmothers thus take on the role not as "Granny," but
as second "Momma." If the parent is working, it is not uncommon
for "Granny" or "Nana" to be responsible for other mothering in the
interim. Much harsher circumstances such as incarceration or drug
addiction quickly conscript grandmother or grandparents into the role
of primary caregiver. To preclude children entering foster care system,
maternal and in some cases paternal mothers bear the onus of rearing
boys and girls.

Teen mothering, although technically not in the other mothering
category, does open the door for a variation of it. Most teenage mothers are not old enough to live by themselves. Many are minors whose
mothers or some guardian are responsible for their care. As a teenaged
mother tries to provide for a child, she herself is also a child in need of
nurture and guidance. Thus the grandmother or guardian of the teen's
baby can easily find herself or himself being responsible for the baby
and the mother of the baby. Thus, there is a coupling aspect to other
mothering.

Whereas teen birth rates are higher among Hispanic and African American adolescent females (respectively 46.3 and 43.9 births
per 1,000), one must note that the national teen pregnancy rate has
declined over the last two decades.[23] Studies cite a higher percentage
of teens are postponing sexual intercourse, with contraception, socio-
economic status, and family structure (presence of both parents) as guiding
factors.[24] Conversely it is also a different understanding of family struc-

23. The Department of Health and Human Services, Office of Adolescent Health, "Trends in Teen Pregnancy and Childbearing," http://www.hhs.gov/ash/oah/adolescent-health-topics/reproductive-health/teen-pregnancy/trends.html#.U6ygsSjxp74.
24. Cheryl Wetzstein, "Study Finds Teens Postponing Sex, Using Birth Control More," *The Washington Times*, http://www.washingtontimes.com/news/2011/oct/12/study-teens-postpone-sex-using-birth-control-more/?page=all.

ture that demonstrates the measures people take to help adolescents who give birth. Family relationships may include multiple generations including the roles of grandparents and great-grandparents. Extended family members are also critical in providing a context to foster successful outcomes for the teens and their offspring.

No one doubts that there is some level of disappointment when a family grapples with an unwanted teenage pregnancy. Yet it is not unusual for a rallying of human and financial resources to "make it work." As families in African American contexts come to terms with the unexpected "I'm expecting" moment, relatives adjust and do what is necessary to prepare for the teen birth. Family relationships play a key role in the lives of pregnant and subsequently parenting teens. Hence the other mothering not only comes to bear after the teenager has given birth, but there is a double, maternal nurturing throughout the pregnancy. Again this presents a different form of other mothering.

Whereas matriarchs and matrifocal families lean toward internal structure and order, other mothering extends the metes and bounds of maternal living. This allows for a more external approach where mothers looks beyond their four walls to include children not their own. This broadening of the family provides a foundation for community activist mothers whose work centers on rectifying the social, political, and economic ills that hinder their settings.

COMMUNITY AND CHURCH MOTHERS: VISION MOTHERS

The year 2014 marked the fiftieth anniversary of Freedom Summer. During this time in 1964 young people from across the United Stated descended on small communities in parts of Mississippi and Alabama to register voters. Leading such groups were women like Fannie Lou Hamer and Ella Baker who began their work as community organizers. These women among many others were seen as the "community mothers" whose vision for a better, just society propelled teens to join the fight. Theirs was not only the responsibility of securing a political future but also ensuring the physical well-being of young activists in the heat of the battle.

Community mothers may or may not have had biological children of their own. Their "seed" was the many women, men, and children who did not have voices to tell of their own economic plight or social hardship. The progeny of the community mothers includes anyone who needs an advocate to cry out against racial discrimination and class prejudice. Marching to the beat of Mary Church Terrell, Nannie Helen Burroughs, and Mary MacLeod Bethune, these activist matriarchs yield a clarion call for a new day and a new order. Cheryl Townsend Gilkes notes, "Community mothers are the guardians of community political traditions. Their ability to function as power brokers stemmed from their leadership within the historical black women's movement and organizations."[25]

What is unique about the community mothers vis-a-vis "other mothers" and matriarchs is that they vocalized their disagreement with systems and structures during times in which African American women had more education, social opportunities, and more freedom. The likes of Burroughs, Bethune, and Dorothy Height were college graduates. Yet they thought it not beneath them to open doors for those who did not have access to such basic human rights. Whereas it was not uncommon for community mothers at the grassroots level to lack formal education, they wielded a common sense to speak to the ills of the day. Thus community mothers included various prototypes, the educated club women who fought through the National Association for the Advancement of Colored People (NAACP) and the National Council of Negro Women. Included were women without formal education who still knew the power of door-to-door mobilization. Both levels of community mothers continue their work of advocacy today.

Related to the community mothers are the church mothers who wield their power in sacred space. The mothers outside of the church tend to have more authority than those who dwell in holy places. Environments of patriarchy are the order of the day in many church settings across denominational lines. Baptist, Church of God in Christ, and Methodist traditions are gravid with sexist theologies that limit what women can and cannot do. The church mother embodies that of the caretaker of the "Body of Christ." This is over against the strong arm community mothers have in nurturing and advocating for the "Body of the Community."

Church mothers are expected to provide meals, assist with planning women's events, and cater to the basic needs of the pastor or bishops. Many are often department heads related to Christian education. They oversee the Women's Convention in addition to being core fundraisers and principle tithers. However, male leaders often limit their service

---

25. Cheryl Townsend Gilkes, *If It Wasn't for the Women* (Maryknoll, NY: Orbis, 2001), 65.

to these functions. Church mothers are rarely evangelists, preachers, pastors, or bishops. If they are serving in such roles, it is due to self-appointment. Gilkes avers, "These varieties of women's power and position indicate clearly that the role of women in ministry and in the hierarchy of African American churches remained a central and critical debate that often fueled the reorganization of social worlds within the black religious experience."[26]

Church mothers and community mothers are indeed mothers of vision. This is not to discount the forward thinking of matriarchs and other mothers. Community mothers tend to think beyond their four walls and focus on demolishing systemic edifices constructed with the bricks of racism and the mortar of poverty. Church mothers, through their subversive work, bring to the surface the erroneous mandates that subjugate women in the church to certain degrees and types of ministry. It is through their work that one sees the dangers of female relegation while also glimpsing what an egalitarian, nonsexist sacred space should entail.

The survey of the African American motherhood is vast and profound. Women of African descent have long held in high esteem their role as mother. In tribes in West Africa rooted in matrilineal and even maternal-rule traditions, motherhood rocks! Although the structures of slavery intended to decapitate family structures, mothers in slavery still were able to provide some sense of family order while having to surrender and perform as mother to the master's seed. The strength of such mothers did not dissipate but was a force that would not yield to the dehumanizing caricatures of mammy even in the Reconstruction. Matrifocal and matriarchal family units developed to counter the capitalistic system's means of castrating men, thus precluding them from being an economic force in the family.

Sister bonds among mothers allow for an atmosphere of other mothering. Women today still help to fill in the gap for each other in whatever maternal means is necessary. While many mothers focus on providing a shelter and putting food on the table, the role of community mother is that of helping to guarantee that all mothers have a job and access to education in order to sustain themselves and their families. Community mothers are free and unrestricted, whereas their visionary counterparts of church mothers tend to minister under more burdened and circumscribed conditions. This history of African

26. Ibid., 72.

American motherhood is as diverse as it is complex and as profound as it is organic. Mothers, you rock!

Questions for Discussion

1. What are some modern-day "mammy" images?
2. Is the idea of "matriarch" good, bad, or both? Why?
3. What connections do you see between African and African American mothers?
4. Is the idea of African American women and mothers being responsible for children who are not their own still a prevalent idea? Why or why not?
5. Name some community mothers in your current context. What makes them "community" mothers?

2

Womanist Maternal Thought

... back to the mothering blackness ...
　　　　　　　—Maya Angelou, "The Mothering Blackness"[1]

Womanist maternal thought examines the ways in which race, class, and gender identity impact the lives of African American mothers. It sheds light on the challenges African American mothers face as women, conditions that tailor their work inside and outside of the home, and the manner in which racism impedes their being. The following stories help to introduce this idea.

Leslye was fired from McDonald's not because she burned burgers or due to bad customer service. Management terminated her because she left her daughter playing in a nearby park while she worked. Leslye maintained she did not neglect the child because the little girl had a cell phone in case of emergencies. Although charges of child endangerment were dropped, the Big Mac dropped Leslye nonetheless.

Jeemira's children slept in the car while she went to a job interview. Someone noticed the children and called the police. Without much questioning, Jeemira was arrested. However, her story went viral. She was not trying to abandon her children. In her mind there was no other recourse but to leave the children in the safety of car. After all, she really needed that job.

Dinah put an ad for a home on Craigslist. She wasn't trying to buy a home. She was seeking shelter for her and her three children.

---

1. Maya Angelou, "The Mothering Blackness," in *The Collected Poems of Maya Angelou* (New York: Random House, 1994), 22.

She worked part time as a nursing assistant, but the pay just was not enough. No homeless shelter had room. So she turned to advertising on the internet in hopes someone would provide covering for her family. However, social services took the children and "found them a home" away from their mother before anyone responded to Dinah's Craigslist plea.

The names in the above cases differ from the real cases.[2] Yes, these are true events. Stories abound of African American mothers needing to work or find work but lacking the benefit of someone—anyone— to watch their babies. Maternal drive pushes women to take unusual measures. No, the aforementioned women and many others in similar desperate states are not bad women. However, the daily grind of living between a rock and a hard place can coerce anyone, even mothers, to act in ways that seem inhumane to outsiders.

Systems of economic exploitation and jobs where minimum wage is paltry force people in general, and mothers especially, to behave in an unorthodox manner. Of course no mother in her "right mind" wants to leave a child in the park or a car, but financial desperation has a way of robbing the most intelligent of her senses. For so many African American mothers, the issue is not male-female inequity; sexism is not on their radar. Paying the rent, having food to eat, and being able to keep the utilities on consistently are their main concerns; classism has a foot on their necks. Leslye, Jeemira, and Dinah may not use the word "classism"; however, they can talk about money issues, finances, lack, bills, and simply not having enough. The vicissitudes of life have taught them well the art of survival. Womanist maternal thought helps to put words to the experiences of these and other working mothers.

GETTING TO WOMANISM

Womanism or womanist thinking scrutinizes race, class, and gender. In her work *Too Heavy a Yoke: Black Women and the Burden of Strength,* Chanequa Walker-Barnes defines womanist thinking as analyses of race, gender, and religion.[3] Further in her work, Walker-Barnes argues that the intersection of race, gender, and class creates a lethal stronghold for

2. "Black Mothers Under Siege," *The Root,* accessed August 5, 2014, http://www.theroot.com/photos/2014/08/black_mothers_under_siege.html.
3. Chanequa Walker-Barnes, "Introduction," *Too Heavy a Yoke: Black Women and the Burden of Strength* (Eugene, OR: Cascade Books, 2014), 8.

black women. Black women's experiences cannot be solely explained by race or gender. Our joys and struggles are quantitatively and qualitatively different from black men, white women, and other women of color.[4]

While examining the idea of the Strong Black Woman, Walker-Barnes explains the tenets of womanist thinking. Womanist thinking is an interpretive approach that takes into account the role of race, gender, and class, among other ontological factors, in the lives of African American women. Womanist hermeneutics interrogates and analyzes the roles assigned to African American or African Diasporan women by their families and the dominant culture, the persistent stereotypes about African American women, the impact of race with gender and class (my addition), and the diversity among women.[5] Delores Williams asserts that a womanist theology challenges all oppressive forces impeding black women's struggle for survival; it affirms the development of a positive, productive quality of life that is conducive to the women's and the families' freedom and well-being.

Alice Walker coined the word "womanist." She chose the term over "black feminist" because she deemed it more reflective of black women's culture, especially Southern culture.[6] Walker employs color play to define womanism as different from feminism:

> Womanist 1. From *womanish*. (Opp. of "girlish," i.e., frivolous, irresponsible, not serious). A black feminist or feminist of color. . . . "You acting womanish," i.e., like a woman. Usually referring to outrageous, audacious, courageous or *willful* behavior. Wanting to know more and in greater depth than is considered "good" for one.
> 2. *Also*: a woman who loves other women, sexually and/or nonsexually. Appreciates and prefers women's culture, . . . and women's strength. . . . Committed to survival and wholeness of entire people, male *and* female. Not a separatist . . . .
> 3. Loves music. Loves dance. Loves the moon. *Loves* the Spirit. Loves love and food and roundness. . . . Loves herself. *Regardless.*
> 4. Womanist is to feminist as purple to lavender.[7]

Using this color analogy, Walker maintains that womanism is a deeper shade of feminism just as purple is a deeper shade of lavender. Chromatic exchange of "deeper shade" is a reference to the ontological

4. Ibid.
5. Stephanie Y. Mitchem, *Womanist Theology* (Maryknoll, NY: Orbis Books, 2002), 23.
6. Alice Walker, "Audre's Voice," in *Anything We Love Can Be Saved: A Writer's Activism* (New York: Random House, 1997), 80.
7. Alice Walker, *In Search of Our Mother's Garden* (Orlando: Harcourt Books, 1983), xi–xii.

nature of womanist. In other words, is it a play on the darker skin of womanists versus the white skin of feminists? Does she suggest that "purple" is better than "lavender"? I do not think this is where Walker pitches her tent. However, I think she posits that there are ways in which the experiences and needs of African American women are not encapsulated in the word "feminism." Thus being the literary artist that she is, Walker presents a new word to speak to the urgent need to address the experiences of black women.

Although Alice Walker first introduced the term "womanism" in 1983, the first development of "womanist" thinking reaches as far back as the nineteenth century with foremothers such as Anna Julia Cooper, Maria Stewart, Virginia Broughton, and Ida B. Wells. In the nineteenth century, they challenged society's oppressive standards and actions related to gender and race.

A second development in womanist thinking appeared during the 1950s and early 1960s in the civil rights movement. What was problematic for "womanist" thinking during this period was the manner in which African American women's issues took a backseat to overall racial progress. The hegemony focused more on getting ahead as a race versus highlighting the subjugation of African American women, despite the intense labor of Fannie Lou Hamer, Ella Baker, Dorothy Cotton, Septima Clark, and other key African American women.

A third development of "womanism" emerged in the late 1970s and 1980s as the feminist movement in the United States was hitting its zenith. Many women, primarily white middle-to-upper-class women, heralded the clarion call of equality with men. However, in the midst of this social and political struggle, some African American women became disgruntled because their issues of racial difference and class displacement became invisible. Additionally, opposing African American women maintained that feminism was too anti-male and lacked expressions of communal wholeness.

There is yet another evolution of womanism. Although taking a theological approach, Monica Coleman's analysis of the dilemma of feminism is still apropos. In her book *Making a Way Out of No Way*, she asserts, "Feminist theologians . . . unwittingly spoke only of white women's experience, especially of middle-and upper-class white women. They did not include issues of race and economics in their critiques. Womanists for the most part assert that feminist thinking operates in opposition to men and is anathema to the church."[8] Coleman,

---

8. Monica Coleman, *Making A Way Out of No Way: A Womanist Theology* (Minneapolis: Fortress Press, 2008), 6.

expounding on various developments within womanism, even pushes the ideological envelope by offering a salient internal critique on its failure to engage in interreligious dialogue and publically speak to political identity.[9] For her, womanism in its current state engages in advocacy and values work and thinkers both inside and outside African American religious scholarship.[10] For the sake of global equity and community womanism in this fourth iteration coerces adherents to seek to do justice with all persons of various sacred traditions. It appears that Coleman challenges womanists to return to aspects of Walker's original definition of womanist as one who simply loves "Spirit."[11]

In many arenas, African American women have challenged or resisted feminism. The challenges include: (1) feminism lacked a "class" agenda; (2) feminism lacked a message for men and women in community; (3) feminism ignored racism; (4) feminist theology did not value religious experience; and (5) feminism ignored issues of gender identity. For African American women dissenting with feminist agendas, Walker's "womanism" gave an impetus to do a new thing. Although many African American women in theology critiqued feminism for its distance from the church, they adopted "womanism" as a mode of study and a way of living. Walker's original definition of womanism bears no explicitly theological or Christian meaning. It states that a womanist "loves the Spirit." She does not define "Spirit." Nonetheless "womanism" became and still is a means by which many African American women could be both African American and female while working for the liberation of all African Americans, especially the poor. According to Rachel St. Clair, "Walker's nomenclature furnished them [African American women]with the language and framework to be who they are and pursue liberation from sexist, racist, classist, and heterosexist oppression."[12]

WOMANIST MATERNAL THOUGHT

Using womanism as a hermeneutical foundation, I expand its metes and bounds and propose a womanist maternal method. This path particularly brings to the surface the voices of mothers within an African American racial, ethnic, spiritual, and sociological context, whether the

9. Monica Coleman, *Ain't I A Womanist Too? Third-Wave Womanist Religious Thought* (Minneapolis: Fortress Press, 2013), 10.
10. Ibid., 19.
11. Walker, *Anything We Love*, xii.
12. Rachel St. Clair, "Womanist Biblical Interpretation," in *True to Our Native Land: An African American New Testament Commentary* (Minneapolis: Fortress Press, 2007), 56.

mothers are biological or women who for some reason took responsibility for and helped to care for another's child. Womanist authors like Teresa Fry Brown, Barbara Essex, and Renita Weems, to name a few, have addressed mother/motherhood, but none under the auspices of a "womanist maternal thinking."[13]

Womanist maternal thought addresses the specific racial context of African American women and the mothering challenges connected to it that are unique to mothers in this social context, and therefore it is not universal. Motherhood among African American women may seem general in comparison to other mothers; however, race and racism compound and complicate their experiences of African American mothers. Just as racial identification shrouds the actions by and perceptions of African American people, it also impacts the existence of African American mothers. As society attempts to demean women's existence and constrict their opportunities, such efforts weigh more heavily stacked against African American women. I maintain that African American mothers not only have to filter through sexist measures and racial roadblocks, but they must also maneuver systemic economic blockades and speed bumps that devalue their familial status. Thus African American women who are mothers have to pummel a triple level of hardship. Furthermore, as corporate arenas (even those that hire the Leslyes) and academic institutions erect monuments of career immobility for women and African Americans, the same obstacles often force African American mothers to choose between career and family.

Therefore, a womanist maternal thought is a tripartite approach to understanding the nature of being African American, woman, and mother. It reveals the organic complexities of women who live, move, and have their being in this ontological, racial, sexual, and familial existence. The stories of Leslye, Jeemira, and Dinah might be different if their race and family composition were different. These three women faced exceptional difficulties as working African American mothers. In attempts to care for their children, to provide housing,

---

13. Stephanie Buckhanon Crowder, "Biblical/Black Mother Working/Wrecking," *Semeia Studies* 61 (November 2009): 157–67. Teresa L. Fry Brown, *God Don't Like Ugly: African American Women Handing on Spiritual Values* (Nashville: Abingdon Press, 2000). Brown talks at length of the importance of African American grandmothers, mothers, and othermothers in handing on spiritual values or moral wisdom across generations of African American families, churches, and communities through their use of biblical mandates, precepts, and examples. Barbara J. Essex, "Some Kind of Woman: The Making of a Strong Black Woman," in *Embracing the Spirit: Womanist Perspectives on Hope, Salvation and Transformation* (Maryknoll, NY: Orbis Books, 1997), pp. 203–11. Essex discusses the role of her grandmother and mother in her childhood and adult life. Renita J. Weems, "My Mother, My Self," in *Showing Mary: How Women Can Share Prayers, Wisdom, and the Blessings of God* (West Bloomfield, MI: Walk Worthy Press, 2002), pp. 117–25. Weems highlights her relationship with her mother and its impact on her own relationship with her daughter.

to be economically dependent, and to sustain a degree of welfare and well-being, the women had jobs outside of the home. Such efforts were more compounded in light of their having to navigate turbulent waters of race, sex, and class.

In addition to analyzing the intersection of race, family, and gender constructions as related to African American mothers, the final thrust of womanist maternal thought is to scrutinize the dynamics of class in their experiences. By underscoring class status and its connection to African American working mothers, this framework examines how work is a determining factor in an African American mother's economic standing. Womanist maternal thinking undergirds work as a core component of the role of African American mothers.

Womanist maternal thought defines work as an activity that brings wholeness and health to children. This work occurs in the home or outside its environs. There is no doubt that stay-at-home mothers labor for the sake of their family. This project will not engage in the debate of "working" mom versus "stay-at-home" mom. It seeks to delineate the general work that each mom does and the challenges that emanate from doing this in African American skin.

Patricia Hill Collins states that understandings of African American women's work were organic. "And whereas African women worked on behalf of their families and children, enslaved African-American women's labor benefited their owners."[14] The beneficiary of the African American woman's labor changed depending on her own social, economic, and political freedom or lack thereof.

Work as alienated labor can be economically exploitative, physically demanding, and intellectually deadening—the type of work long associated with African American women's status as "mule."[15] Yet work can also be empowering and creative, even if it is physically challenging and appears to be the labor of the lower class. Exploitative wages that African American women were allowed to keep and use for their own benefit or labor done out of love for members of one's own family can represent such work.[16]

Instead of conceptualizing work by typology, perhaps the motivation and the range of work are better indicators of value and worth. Too often those who earn better salaries with excessive fringe benefits and stock options easily attach self-worth with self-work. Using Collins

14. Patricia Hill Collins, *Black Feminist Thought*, 2nd ed. (New York: Routledge, 2000), 49.
15. Zora Neale Hurston, *Their Eyes Were Watching God* (New York: HarperCollins, 2000), 17.
16. Ibid.

and a broader African American context, the work of mothers who clean the academic halls to survive, heal, and become whole is just as valuable as the work of mothers who teach in the same academic halls for survival, healing, and wholeness.

Feminist thinker Bonnie Miller-McLemore maintains that the dilemma facing working mothers is the struggle between the pro-creative and the creative.[17] It is the tension between wanting to and needing to be mother and yet wanting to and needing to be someone else and being both/and all the time. It is the desire to be at home, at school events, at dance lessons, or athletic events and the desire to write scholarly articles, teach classes, and attend professional meetings. It is a rope that pulls in at least two ways. It is "I am also a mother" language.[18] In addition to who I am as professor, executive, doctor, cook, nurse, teacher, lawyer, maid, clerk, lover, wife, sister—I am also a mother.

The history of African American working mothers cannot be discarded. "Also a mother" were the slave women who nursed master's children and picked and chopped in his fields; then, they went to make a home for their own families. "Also a mother" were two million women of the Reconstruction period who were the earliest house-wives or stay-at-home moms. Reconstruction laws or African American Codes forced many of these post-slavery mothers from their homes back into the fields.[19] Also, African American mothers who migrated to northern factories took in laundry and took in children before there was an official cleaning business or KinderKare. Yes, they were "also a mother." One cannot forget the triple consciousness of family, work, and community exemplified by clubwomen like Ida B. Wells and Mary Church Terrell. As African American women and African American mothers, they did not relinquish their public duty. Wells "nursed her two sons, taking them on trains on the way to her lectures."[20] The story of African American motherhood did not begin here in the United States, but it has its roots in Africa. The close bond between African American women and children "did not lose its importance when African women were brought to America and enslaved."[21]

17. Bonnie Miller-McLemore, *Also a Mother: Work and Family as Theological Dilemma* (Nashville: Abingdon Press, 1994), 91.
18. Ibid.
19. Lonnae O'Neal Parker, *I'm Every Woman: Remixed Stories of Marriage, Motherhood and Work* (New York: HarperCollins, 2005), 33
20. Ibid.
21. Delores S. Williams, *Sisters in the Wilderness: The Challenge of Womanist God-Talk* (New York: Orbis Books, 1993), 34.

Consequently, African American women and mothers have a history of work. Yet now the relevance of such work, and perhaps in some ways this history, is being challenged by the so-called mommy wars. There is a conflict between mothers who stay at home with their children and mothers who work. Of course there are benefits to both sides. There are exceptions to both sides. Stay-at-home moms are the primary soother and coddler and are there for benchmark moments. Children of stay-at-home moms do not necessarily have the separation anxiety experienced in daycare transition. Children of working moms benefit from having a broader social circle with daycare workers, other children, or babysitters. Working mothers also stay in their projected career paths.[22]

There are also drawbacks to each argument. Working mothers may experience guilt over missing a first walk or first word. For children, even the most sanitized daycares breed germs. Children are likely to attract colds and other illnesses from each other. Stay-at-home mothers deal with professional isolation, and the children obviously tend to be more attached to the mothers.[23] Again, there are exceptions to both sides.

Does this mean that mothers who stay at home with their children are happy with their lives? Some are. Some are not. Does this mean that children of stay-at-home mothers are healthier or have a greater mother-child bond? Sometimes yes and sometimes no. Are children of working moms more socially developed? Are these working mothers climbing the corporate ladder with family in tow? I think the answers lie in each of our own lives and what "works" best in our own family situations. There are no absolutes, as perpetrators of these mommy wars would have us believe. In both cases it is evident that both sets of mothers act in their children's best interest.

Generally, African American women, mothers or not, have always worked and will continue to work. Some of the children who come from such homes are the most articulate, independent, socially adept, intellectually sound, and spiritually grounded persons. Yet some children struggle. I cannot say what the defining line or determining factor is or is not. I do not think that work in the sense that I have defined it wrecks the lives of children. Yes, they may miss their mommy, and, yes, mommy may miss an event or two. However, quantity of times present cannot be judged against quality time. I believe to each her own—to each mother, her own. She must use whatever "works" for her. It will work, if one works it.

22. Sheri Spink-Palmieri, "Working vs. Stay at Home." *Babytalk*, February 2006, 54–56.
23. Ibid.

A womanist maternal approach to thinking, conversation, and action does not seek to elevate the experiences of African American mothers over against those of mothers situated in other racial locations. It does not suggest that because a mother is not African American, then she is excluded from this discussion or community. It does not argue that African American mothers face more quandaries than a Latina, white, or Jewish mother.

On the contrary, this mode of interpretation avows that a mother who is African American has to live and act through a certain lens that mothers in other racial and ethnic groups do not, simply because society sees and labels her "African American" or "black." At the same time, a womanist maternal approach does not purport that all African American mothers have the same challenges or opportunities. Suggesting that a one size fits all for African American mothers makes us guilty of seeking a social universality that collapses all humans into the same state of affairs.

Class distinctions exist among African American mothers that tailor the outcome of their lives. The reasons a number of African American mothers work outside of the home range from professional fulfillment, identity outside of the home, or answering a sense of calling or vocation. In such instances, some African American mothers do not need to work for financial stability. On the contrary, other African American mothers struggle to ascertain the bare necessities of life and find themselves conscripted to work jobs not out of professional satisfaction but in order to satisfy basic human needs. The statistics vary concerning African American mothers who want to work versus those who need to work. In this regard, working mothers must come to the defense of other working mothers, as all work is not equal. I affirm Coleman's thinking that a current wave of womanist thought must also maintain a goal of justice, survival, freedom, liberation, and/or quality of life.[24]

CONCLUSION

Womanist maternal thinking offers an external critique of the systemic forces that make it difficult for African American mothers to achieve and sustain social, racial, political, and economic freedom. It disrobes and lays bare oppressive structures seeking to force such

---

24. Coleman, *Ain't I a Womanist Too?*, 21.

mothers to choose between making a living and making a home. Thus classism is an element in this ideological lens. As an approach to redefining work as not only physical labor but also advocacy, womanist maternal thought stands on the shoulders of a community of mothers who stood in the gap for communities of women and their children not able to stand by themselves. The interpretative mode in the legacy of Wells, Bethune, and Terrell dares to challenge and moves to dismantle sexism within the dominant culture. As African American mothers wade through turbid waters of sexism, womanist maternal thought must include this oppression in the conversation. Furthermore, womanist maternal thought addresses the complexity that racism creates in the experiences of African American mothers.

Additionally, womanist maternal thought calls on the carpet external factors exacerbating the existence of African American mothers. It does so through an internal exchange contesting any lack of "sister-motherly" regard. In other words this ideology conscripts privileged African American mothers of comfortable fiscal means to attend to and champion the cause of the their sisters who must work or die. This lifting as we climb through speech and fight provides a forum for community and accountability. It is the maternal epitome of "Ubuntu"—I am because we are. I am a better African American mother only as you, Leslye, Jeemira, and Dinah are better African American mothers.

Questions for Discussion

1. What are your earliest images of motherhood?
2. Should an African American mother work? How do you define "work"?
3. What does womanist maternal thinking mean to you?
4. What is the role of men in connection with womanist maternal thought?
5. What are the pros and cons of being an African American mother?

3

Womanist Biblical Interpretation

O, ye mothers, what a responsibility rests on you!
—Maria W. Stewart[1]

The late educator and philosopher Howard Thurman tells the experience of reading the Bible to his grandmother. He records that she welcomed recitations from any of the biblical literature except the epistles of Paul. His grandmother, who was born a slave and lived until the Civil War, chided him that the slave masters always lifted Paul's words on slavery in order ensure compliance. "Since the Bible says 'Slaves obey your masters,' then slavery was God's will," would be the white plantation preacher's excuse. For this reason Thurman's grandmother was selective in her Scripture engagement.[2]

Before the term "womanist" existed within literary or theological circles, African American women were already reading and quoting the Bible. The story of Thurman's grandmother illustrates that women of African descent are not new to reading the Bible. This does not mean that all women of an African hue engage the biblical text. The idea of African American women interpreting the Scriptures precedes any naming of the act. In other words, Thurman's grandmother may not have known much about womanist thinking or hermeneutics, yet she knew that race and class status are conversation partners with reading and interpreting the Bible.

African American women activist pioneers such as Harriet Tubman,

---

1. Maria W. Stewart, "Maria Stewart," in *Black Women in Nineteenth-Century American Life*, ed. Bert Lowenberg and Ruth Bogin (University Park: Pennsylvania State University Press, 1991), 188.
2. Howard Thurman, *Jesus and the Disinherited* (Boston: Beacon Press, 1976), 30–31.

Sojourner Truth, and Amanda Berry Smith are a few whose images or speeches ring with biblical references. The comparison of Harriet Tubman to the Moses of the book of Exodus recalls her work to free slaves just as he led God's people out of Egyptian bondage.[3] References to the Scriptures are in the works of Sojourner Truth and Amanda Berry.[4] For Anna Julia Cooper, Frances Ellen Watkins Harper, and Ida B. Wells, who followed their paths, the Bible served as justification for "lifting as we climb."[5]

Time will not permit an extensive review of these and other women who were engaging in "womanist" interpretations with the biblical text. However, a brief excursus of three of the earliest examples is necessary for providing background for what is currently coined womanist biblical interpretation. Maria W. Stewart, Jarena Lee, and Elizabeth, are three African American female literary activists and lecturers in a pre-womanist era whose works I examine because they are the earliest publications noting the connections of race, class, gender, and the Bible—the core of womanist biblical interpretation.

READING LIKE A "WOMANIST"
BEFORE THERE WAS "WOMANISM"

The above quote from Maria W. Stewart in 1832 is a testament to the ways in which African American women were reading the Bible prior to any academic naming for what they were doing. Stewart is referencing Jeremiah 9:1, as the prophet laments his people's condition in Babylonian exile. Born in 1803, Stewart was one of the earliest African American female public theologians. Yet others, whose births preceded hers, published after Stewart. Although she did not refer to herself or even view her actions through a womanist interpretive lens, her speeches are replete with biblical language and its connections to race, class, and gender. Speaking through political discourse about racial progress, she often quoted the Bible.

3. Harriet Tubman, *Africans in America*, http://www.pbs.org/wgbh/aia/part4/4p1535.html
4. Amanda Berry Smith, *An Autobiography. The Story of the Lord's Dealings With Mrs. Amanda Smith: The Colored Evangelist; Containing an Account of Her Life Work of Faith, . . . and Africa, as an Independent Missionary*, (Washington, DC: CreateSpace Independent Publishing Platform), 2013. Sojourner Truth, "Ain't I A Woman?" http://www.sojournertruth.org/Library/Speeches/AintIAWoman.htm.
5. Beverly Guy-Sheftall, ed., *Words of Fire: An Anthology of African-American Feminist Thought* (New York: Norton Publishing), 1995, "The Status of Woman in America" by Anna Julia Cooper; "Woman's Political Future" by Frances Ellen Watkins Harper; "Lynch Law in America" by Ida B. Wells. Guy-Sheftall's work is a collection of writings and speeches from Anna Julia Cooper, Frances Ellen Watkins Harper, and Ida B. Wells, among other African American pre-feminist and pre-womanist leaders.

Stewart uses the Bible to urge her listeners not to allow societal or class status to limit their political and social abilities. In an 1831 document, "Religion and the Pure Principles of Morality," where she connects the role of faith in action, Stewart lifts portions of Psalm 46: "Then, my brethren, sheath your swords and calm your angry passions. Stand still and know that the lord he is God. Vengeance is his and he will repay. It is a long lane that has no turn."[6] The same work includes a reference to Psalm 8, "He hath crowned you with glory and honor and hath made you a little lower than the angels."[7] A call to fight against racial injustice and an awareness of self-worth are at the heart of Stewart's words.

Stewart's farewell address to the city of Boston in 1833 takes a more generalist approach to incorporating biblical texts with women's political activism:

> Is not the God of the ancient times, the God of these modern times? Did not queen Esther save the lives of the Jews? And Mary Magdalene first declare the resurrection of Christ from the dead? St. Paul declared that it was a shame for a woman to speak in public, yet our great High Priest and Advocate did not condemn the woman for a more notorious offence than this. . . .[8]

As she is discontinuing her public work, Stewart makes one final plea for her listeners to move forward with women's work. Stewart references gender dynamics to address issues pertaining to race within a certain politically rife context.

In both speeches Stewart does not shy away from employing biblical texts in conjunction with race, class, and gender talk. She situates her speeches within this tripartite approach and makes use of the Bible for theological framing, which is indicative of womanist biblical interpretation insofar as the social "who-ness" of African American women along with class consciousness comes to bear in reading this sacred text.

Jarena Lee's engagement of the Bible with social identity follows a similar trajectory as Stewart's. Although Lee was born in 1783, almost twenty years before Stewart, the first record of her work is in 1849, fifteen years after Stewart's first documented speech. In "Giving an Account of Her Call to Preach the Gospel," Lee recounts her experiences to live into her call to preach. She reveals wrestling with African

---

6. Stewart, "Maria Stewart," 191.
7. Ibid.
8. Stewart, "Maria Stewart," in ibid., 198.

Methodist Episcopal denominational officials, particularly its founder, Richard Allen, about her calling.[9] Lee quotes the Bible to substantiate a woman's call to preach:

> If the man may preach, because the Saviour died for him, why not the woman? Seeing he died for her also. Is he not a whole Saviour, instead of a half one? Did not Mary first preach the risen Savior, and is not the doctrine of the resurrection the very climax of Christianity—hangs not all our hope on this as argued by St. Paul. Then did not Mary, a woman preach the gospel?[10]

She positions the text with gender to affirm a woman's religious role and right. Later she brings to the surface issue of class by highlighting that the disciples, although they were "fishermen and ignorant of letters," were inspired to preach.[11]

Lee notes that she was a widow with infant children as she fought to answer God's call. She left her children with other women in her community while she traveled through the country preaching. The streams of womanist biblical interpretation and even womanist maternal thought are evident in Jarena Lee's autobiographical account.

Addressing her experiences as a woman called to preach, Elizabeth makes a move akin to Lee. Born in 1766, almost fifteen years before Lee and forty years before Stewart, Elizabeth's published works did not surface until 1889. Unlike Jarena Lee and Maria W. Stewart, history does not record a last name for "Elizabeth." In some texts she is simply "Old" or "Ole" Elizabeth.[12]

Elizabeth also employs biblical passages to address personal and communal progress. She discusses preaching experiences in a similar vein to Lee: "At a meeting which I held in Maryland, I was led to speak from the passage, 'Woe to the rebellious city (Zephaniah 3:1).' After the meeting the people came to take me to squire, but the Lord delivered me from their hands . . . I was led at different times to converse with white men."[13] She not only reflects on attempts to harm her person, but she holds the community responsible for its own circumstances.

In true prophetic form, Elizabeth expounds on her attempt to bring awareness to communal wrongdoing and the ensuing rejection and

9. Ibid., 141.
10. Jarena Lee, "Religious Experience and Journal of Mrs. Jarena Lee, Giving an Account of Her Call to Preach the Gospel," in ibid., 137.
11. Ibid.
12. Elizabeth, "Elizabeth, A Colored Minister of the Gospel, born in Slavery," in ibid., 133.
13. Ibid.

harm that almost followed. Some of the potential danger emanated
due to her gender and some due to her race. She speaks of John in
Revelation to refute her white male opponents questioning her interpretation.[14] For Elizabeth holds white people in general at fault for
what white men attempt to do to her and to others in her community.

While not much else is known of her writings, this brief summary
helps to show how Elizabeth juxtaposed biblical language in her efforts
to speak to the ills of her community. The Bible was also a resource for
her validating her call to ministry and engaging in racial debates. Again,
like Lee and Stewart, the merging of race, gender, and class through
the lens of the biblical mandate are evident in the self-revealing work
of Elizabeth. Though Elizabeth's writings are sparse, they shed light on
the earliest approaches to womanist biblical thinking. Whereas she did
not write under this specific mode of interpretation, her use of biblical
texts to speak to race, gender, and class helps to create an early continuum for womanism and the bible.

The works of Maria W. Stewart, Jarena Lee, and Elizabeth elucidate
the concept of womanism as a mode of interpretation that forms over-
lapping circles of race, class, and gender. These women had no knowledge or awareness of the term "womanist." However, they engaged
not only in womanist interpretation but also in womanist biblical
hermeneutics. They used the word and speech to lift the intersection of
race, class, and gender, and the Bible was their foundation for peering
through this interpretive window. Through racialized, gendered, and
class-conscious perspectives, Stewart, Lee, and Elizabeth set the biblical
text as influencing their respective communal and personal context.

READING THE BIBLE UNDER THE BANNER OF WOMANISM

The idea of womanism as a literary mode of interpretation began with
Alice Walker's declaration in the 1970s. Around the 1990s, womanism
entered into biblical studies with the first wave of African American
women with PhDs in Hebrew Bible/Old Testament and New Testament studies. Blazing the trail were Renita Weems (Hebrew Bible/Old
Testament) and Clarice Martin (New Testament). Scholars engaging
in womanist biblical interpretation in the 2000s, almost a decade later,
include Raquel St. Clair, Nyasha Junior, Shannel Smith, Mitzi Smith,

14. Ibid., 134.

and Wil Gafney.[15] I realize there is danger in naming or not naming folk. These scholars are of note because to date they have published works that include "womanist" in some form or another. Time will not allow discussion of all the catalogs from my sister scholars.[16] Not all African American women biblical scholars write under the umbrella of "womanism."

Although Renita Weems does not use "womanist" in her article "African American Women and the Bible," she explores "ways that factors in American society (associated with gender, race, and in some cases, class) have shaped African American women's relationship with the Bible."[17] This seminal work on the topic from 1991 provides socio-historical analysis of how African American women have encountered the Bible. Weems also provides brief exegetical commentaries on biblical texts. She sets the contextual framework that has influenced how African American women read the Bible and with studies on Hagar (Gen. 16 and 21) and Onesimus (Phlm. 1:16–17) providing examples of such readings.

Clarice Martin defines a womanist as "a black feminist (or feminist of color) who claims her roots in black history, religion, and culture."[18] In her essay "The Haustafeln (Household Codes) in African American Biblical Interpretation: 'Free Slaves' and 'Subordinate Women,'" this definition is the basis of her analysis of the household codes in the Bible (Col. 3:22–25; Eph. 6:5–8; 1 Pet. 2:18–25). According to Martin, "A womanist reflection on the hermeneutical paradoxes, issues, and tensions in the slave-woman regulation in the Haustafeln takes seriously . . . guidelines for the dismantling of the hierarchy of African American

---

15. Rachel St. Clair, "Womanist Biblical Interpretation," in *True to Our Native Land: An African American New Testament Commentary* (Minneapolis: Fortress Press, 2007); Shanell T. Smith, *The Woman Babylon and the Marks of Empire: Reading Revelation with a Postcolonial Womanist Hermeneutics of Ambiveilence* (Minneapolis: Fortress Press, 2014); Mitzi Smith, *I Found God in Me: A Womanist Biblical Hermeneutics Reader* (Eugene: Cascade Books, 2015); Nyasha Junior, *Introduction to Womanist Biblical Interpretation* (Louisville, KY: Westminster John Knox Press, 2015); Wil Gafney, *Womanist Midrash: A Reintroduction to the Women of the Torah and the Throne* (Louisville, KY: Westminster John Knox Press, forthcoming).

16. Here is a sampling of works that include womanist biblical interpretation: Cheryl Anderson, *Ancient Laws and Contemporary Controversies: The Need for Inclusive Interpretation* (New York: Oxford University Press, 2009); Stephanie Buchanon Crowder, *Simon of Cyrene: A Case of Roman Conscription* (New York: Peter Lang, 2002). Kelly Brown Douglas, "Marginalized People, Liberating Perspectives: A Womanist Approach to Biblical Interpretation," *The Anglican Theological Review*, 83 no. 1 (2001): 41–48. Wilda Gafney. "Translation Matters: A Fem/Womanist Exploration of Translation Theory and Practice for Proclamation in Worship," SBL Forum, http://www.sbl-site.org/assets/pdfs/gafney.pdf. Koala Jones-Warsaw. "Toward a Womanist Hermeneutic: A Reading of Judges 19–21," *Journal of the Interdenominational Theological Center* 22 (1994): 18–35.

17. Renita J. Weems, "African American Women and the Bible," in *Stony the Road We Trod: African American Biblical Interpretation*, Cain Hope Felder, ed. (Minneapolis: Fortress Press, 1991), 59.

18. Clarice J. Martin, "The Haustafeln (Household Codes) in African American Biblical Interpretation: 'Free Slaves' and 'Subordinate Women,'" in *Stony the Road We Trod: African American Biblical Interpretation*, Cain Hope Felder, ed. (Minneapolis: Fortress Press, 1991), 227.

men and women."[19] For Martin womanists approaching the Bible
seek to uncover the ways in which this sacred text is used to validate
female oppression at the hands of men in the church and in society.
Her commentary on the husband-wife, parent-child, and master-child
relationships in the Bible provide the base for her reviewing current-
day male-female dynamics.

Raquel St. Clair's is the first monograph under the auspices of womanist biblical interpretation. Prior to it, only essays and articles had
been written, but not an entire book based solely on womanism and
biblical hermeneutics. St. Clair purports that the "social, economic,
political, and spiritual location of African American women neces-
sitates a theological perspective that seriously considers gender, race,
and class and the interplay among them."[20] With this foundation, she
describes Mark's discipleship as that which involves the cross, suffer-
ing, call, and consequences. Combining her womanist approach with
macrolinguistic studies, St. Clair's reading of this Gospel allows African
American women to access honor through discipleship and militates
being a "baby's mama" as honorable.[21] The author teeters with what I
call womanist maternal thinking.

A postcolonial womanist reading of Revelation adds to the pool of
womanist biblical interpretation. Shanell Smith presents an "ambiveilent" perspective on the woman or whore of Babylon in the Apocalypse
of John. For Smith, womanist biblical hermeneutics includes commonalities such as: multidimensionality, the prioritization of women's
experiences, the eradication of human oppression, and accessibility
to nonspecific, wider worship communities.[22] With this framework,
Smith posits the whore of Babylon (Revelation 17–18) as a victim of
two "Johns."[23] Like St. Clair, who combines her womanist approach
with macrolinguistic studies, Smith partners her womanist thinking with postcolonial ideology.[24] Thus, her construction of the word

19. Ibid., 228.
20. Raquel A. St. Clair, *Call and Consequences: A Womanist Reading of Mark* (Minneapolis: Fortress Press, 2008), 17.
21. Ibid., 166.
22. Shanell T. Smith, *The Woman Babylon and the Marks of Empire: Reading Revelation with a Postcolonial Womanist Hermeneutics of Ambiveilence* (Minneapolis: Fortress Press, 2014), 36. Smith constructs the word "ambiveilence."
23. Ibid., 143.
24. I also combine womanist biblical interpretation with other methods in *Simon of Cyrene: A Case of Roman Conscription* (New York: Peter Lang, 2002). Here I engage historical and narrative criticisms along with ideological studies, to aver Simon as one compelled to carry the cross of Jesus due to his context, racial category, and geo-graphical marginalization.

"ambiveilent," a play on the word, "ambivalent," helps to address the layers of gender, race, class, and postcolonial construction.

From one Smith to another is a womanist biblical hermeneutic found in Mitzi Smith's "Knowing More Than Is Good for One." In this essay Smith offers the following on womanism as the core for her discussion of Matthew's Great Commission:

> A womanist who knows "more than is 'good' for one, and in greater depth" is aware that traditional interpretation of sacred texts and interpretive frameworks constructed by malestream biblical scholars and religious specialists, including missionaries, primarily serve the self-interest of men and the white majority.[25]

Smith takes a different section of Walker's womanist definition to discuss how African American mothers teach their children that they have to know more than the status quo. Instead of using the oft-quoted "womanist is to feminist as purple is to lavender" from Alice Walker,[26] Smith borrows "wanting to know more and in greater depth than is considered 'good' for one" from her.[27] For Smith, children must know their place at home and out in the streets. Knowing when to speak and when not to speak can literally save a child's life. Smith uses this understanding of parent-child lessons and knowing when to know in order to challenge imperialistic activity and implementation surrounding the Bible's command to "teach, baptize and teach to the utmost ends of the earth" (Matthew 20:18-20).[28]

The most recent work on womanist biblical interpretation is by Nyasha Junior. She too surveys the authors previously mentioned here. Yet Junior spends too much time contrasting womanist and feminist biblical interpretation. She avers that "womanist biblical interpretation does not have any clearly identifiable common features, than some mention of Walker and the personal identification of the scholar herself."[29] Furthermore, "womanist biblical interpretation does not

25. Mitzi Smith, "Knowing More Than Is Good for One," in *Teaching All the Nations: Interrogating the Matthean Great Commission*, ed. Mitzi J. Smith and Jayachitra Lalitha (Minneapolis: Fortress Press, 2014), 134.

26. Alice Walker, *In Search of Our Mother's Gardens* (San Diego : Harcourt Brace Jovanovich, 1983), xii. Mitzi Smith, "Knowing More Than Is Good for One," in *Teaching All the Nations: Interrogating the Matthean Great Commission*, ed. Mitzi J. Smith and Jayachitra Lalitha (Minneapolis: Fortress Press, 2014), xi.

27. Smith, *Teaching All the Nations: Interrogating the Matthean Great Commission*, xi.

28. Ibid.

29. Junior, *Introduction to Womanist Biblical Interpretation*, 120.

have clear definition . . . and has had minimal impact on the discipline of biblical studies so far."[30]

I take issue with Junior on these fronts. As the aforementioned scholars consistently self-identity and engage Walker, those are features of womanist biblical interpretation. The race-class-gender triad lends toward definition. Additionally I think over twenty-five years of publication by African American women in the field of biblical studies is sand in the eye of the "minimal impact" argument. That Junior quotes women like Weems and Martin, whose seminal work planted the seeds of this discourse, contradicts her own argument. The perpetual impact lies in the fact that biblical studies progeny, including Junior, cannot discuss womanist biblical interpretation without giving honor where honor is due. Womanist biblical interpretation does not begin with Junior's sole work on the topic but has its roots in those who paved the way for the road we now travel.

CONCLUSION

Centuries separated Weems from Stewart, St. Clair from Lee, and Martin from Elizabeth. Even decades separate first-generation African American women biblical scholars from those whose works are now hot off the presses. Yet time does not dilute or years lessen the common strands of African American women's interpretation of the Bible.

First, all of the approaches are contextual because they do not engage the Bible in a vacuum. The interpretation of the texts is rooted in the womanist's context. The current setting provides the backdrop for engaging the Bible and the context that gave rise to "thus saith the Lord." In other words the content and manner of the first generation womanist biblical scholars like Martin and Weems is different from what drove the work of St. Clair and the Smiths. It is not rocket science—all interpretation, including womanist biblical thinking, is setting sensitive.

Second, womanist biblical interpretation holds gender dynamics, race matters, and class systems to the light. African American women see the biblical text as that which liberates the oppressed and lightens the burdens of the dispossessed. Their interpretation of biblical text cleared away any authoritative challenges pertaining to a woman's right to preach and constructively engaged anything forced that hindered her right to just be.

30. Ibid., 121.

Third, womanist biblical interpretation is confrontational. It seeks to antagonize and agitate any unjust society and unethical activity. It even challenges the biblical text itself when its context does not speak overtly or subliminally to the reader in her current-day setting. This hermeneutical approach is a type of ideological sandpaper for a text that is millennia removed from its present-day readers. It can rub the reader the wrong way. Yet twenty-first-century, flesh-and-blood, real readers still choose to engage the Scriptures.

Lastly, womanist biblical interpretation is not monolithic. As each African American woman who chooses to read the Bible brings to the table a different set of experiences, ideas, agendas, and practices, the outcome of their engagement differs. Whereas race, gender, and class triangulate this methodology, the path that respective authors, readers, and interpreters use to draw this triangle is different and subjective. Womanist biblical interpretation is as organic as the people and time that produce it.

Questions for Discussion

1. What does the word "womanist" mean to you?
2. Discuss your experience with reading, hearing, or interpreting the Bible, if you have had any such experience.
3. What do you think makes the ways African American women read and interpret the Bible unique? What makes these acts similar to women of other racial and ethnic groups?
4. Of the definitions of womanist biblical interpretation discussed in this chapter, which most aligns with your identity?
5. Describe your method for reading and interpreting the Bible or any sacred text.

PART TWO

Revealing the Characters

4

Hagar: A Homeless Mother

Genesis 16 and 21:8–21

The relations between the white men and the slave women naturally
aroused the jealousy and antagonism of the women of the master race.
—E. Franklin Frazier[1]

In "Hagar and Her Children," from his classic work *The Negro Family
in the United States,* historian and sociologist E. Franklin Frazier discusses the prevalence of sexual encounters between the slave master and
female slaves. Such liaisons often pitted the slave master's wife against
the slave.[2] Frazier avers: "The relations between the white men and
the slave women naturally aroused the jealousy and antagonism of the
women of the master race."[3] In some cases the slave master's inability
to control his desires for slave women compelled him to act brutally
toward them as well.

This love-hate, hate-lust relationship is evident in the movie *12 Years
a Slave.* The movie is based on Solomon Northup's autobiographical account of his entrapment. Both movie and book provide horri-
ble details of the sexual and physical hardship female slaves endured.
Regarding Patsey, a favorite slave of Master Epps, Northup states, "Her
back bore the scars of a thousand stripes; not because she was backward
in her work, nor because she was an unmindful and rebellious spirit,
but because it had fallen to her lot to be the slave of a licentious master
and a jealous mistress."[4]

An example of Master Epps's (played by Michael Fassbender) licen-
tiousness in the movie is the gut-wrenching scene of him slapping

---

1. E. Franklin Frazier, *The Negro Family in the United States* (Chicago: University of Chicago Press, 1968), 67.
2. Ibid., 68.
3. Ibid., 69.
4. Solomon Northup, *Twelve Years a Slave* (London: Sampson Low and Company, 1853), 77.

Patsey (played by Oscar-winning actress Lupita Nyong'o) as he rapes her.

Frazier's reference to Hagar and her children is a biblical one. Chapters in the book of Genesis record the saga of Hagar, Abraham, and Sarah. The biblical text disrobes elements of the master-slave-wife tryst. There is no indication that Abraham rapes Hagar or makes her subject to any physical abuse. However, the Bible is clear of the traumatic triangle involving Abraham-Hagar-Sarah. Hagar's position as slave, Sarah's barrenness, and Abraham's patriarchal acquiescence make for a perfect storm.

Whereas Hagar does not endure whips or beating, she does suffer an economic disadvantage as the slave woman. Although such insight is not historically new or unexpected, its presence in the Bible may be surprising. It is profound that the Bible, a sacred text to so many, illuminates a love-hate, hate-lust conundrum. Scripture is not shy in proffering how this conflicting master-slave-wife dynamic leaves the most vulnerable, in this case, the slave woman and her seed, homeless.

TEXT SUMMARY

(Genesis 16; Genesis 21:8–21)

Genesis 16 records that Abram and Sarai are without children. This version of the Abram-Hagar-Sarai tryst is from the Yahwist, or J version.[5] In short, biblical scholars think there are two versions of the same story. One written by perhaps some author who uses "Lord" in most cases. The other author uses primarily "God" in reference to the Divine. The name of the Divine as "Lord" is what primarily distinguishes this version from the Genesis 21 story. Although the Lord assures them that their childless state is not permanent (Gen. 15), Sarai takes matters into her own hands and suggests that Abram, at eighty-six years of age, have sex with her Egyptian slave, Hagar. Abram agrees. Hagar conceives. Trouble begins. Hagar knows that she has something old Sarai lacks, a seed for the man of the house. Sarai tells Abram to do something about disrespectful Hagar. She goes a step further and states that if he does not handle it, the Lord will. Abram retorts, "She is your girl, not mine."

---

5. Many biblical scholars purport that there were four editors of the first fives books of the Bible, the Pentateuch. They are J, E, D, and P: J—Jahwist (900–800 BCE), E—Elohist (800–700 BCE), D—Deuteronomic (600 BCE), and P—Priestly (500–400 BCE). See Barry Bandstra, *Reading the Old Testament* (Los Angeles: Wadsworth, 2009).

Sarai is so cruel to Hagar that Hagar runs away with child in utero. Hagar is pregnant and now homeless.

However, the Lord convinces Hagar to return and yield to her mistress with the promise that things will fare well for both her and her seed. The child's name, "the Lord hears," is a sign of the promise Hagar receives as a homeless, single mother. She is without a home now, but the Lord assures her of a mighty nation through her son Ishmael. In the interim, until her appointed time, she must dwell in a house that is not her home.

Fast forward fourteen years and Hagar, Ishmael, and Sarah are back at the ranch. This Genesis 21 story is the Elohist version of the saga. The literary distinctives are the name changes from the matriarch and patriarch. Here, the "Lord" is now "God." Since then, God has reminded and promised Sarai, now "Sarah," and Abram, called "Abraham," that they too will be parents (Gen. 17). Not only will Abraham and Sarah have offspring, but they will have land and blessings in great abundance. In addition, the physical act of circumcision is the external manifestation of this divine covenant. The proof is in the (fore) skin.

Things do not go well back at Abraham's tent. Sarah still has unresolved issues (Gen. 21). Although she and Abraham have the son God promised, Isaac, playing with his brother Ishmael, rubs Sarah the wrong way. Hagar and her child must go—again!

In a conversation almost parallel to the one fourteen years prior, Sarah accosts Abraham to handle Hagar. The current drama is not connected to Hagar being haughty toward Sarah but is rooted in Sarah's insecurity over her son's future security. Ishmael, born of a slave, will not share the inheritance of her son. To put it in vernacular terms, "Abraham, the baby daddy of Ishmael and Isaac, must intervene and fix the mess one baby momma created. The core of the matter is one baby momma not wanting to share the goods with another baby momma."

Genesis 21 notes that Hagar does not run away this time. She is expunged, cast out from among Abraham's people by the patriarch himself. He gives her bread and water, unlike his material disregard in Genesis 16. Yet this meager offering does not assuage Hagar's emotional toil or spiritual turmoil. She thinks both she and her son will die and pleads to God for mercy. This time it is not "the Lord who hears" that comforts; the "God who sees" is the source of assurance. God rescues Hagar and her son with more water and reminds her that God is as good as God's promise. The story ends with Ishmael thriving. Hagar finds him a wife from Egypt. Hagar is homeless no more.

HAGAR THEN

The story of Hagar, Abram/Abraham, and Sarai/Sarah is convoluted to say the least. It is a multilayered problem centered around motherhood. Sarai wants to be a mother. Hagar is the conduit to fulfill Sarai's maternal longing. Hagar has no choice in carrying out what Sarai is choosing to do and to become. While the actions and responses are complex and in some ways disheartening, how these three interact is indicative of their historical context. The narrator of Genesis clearly wants to paint a picture of the slave-master-wife relationship. It is evident that Hagar is not her own and her social and class identity merge with her economic status. Hagar is a displaced, homeless slave who becomes a homeless mother. Yet she wields much power. She is a complex character.

The different personalities of Hagar are perchance attributed to the distinct editors J and E. The J (Yahwist) holds a Hagar yielding much effrontery and gall. John Waters, an Old Testament researcher, states, "In J, she is a bold, proud, resolute Egyptian woman who will not allow herself to be treated harshly by her mistress. Upon becoming pregnant, she assumes equality with Sarai."[6] Although not the wife, she takes the role of the wife in that she is able to do for Abram what Sarai cannot do: bear him a child. Hagar exudes further control by deciding to run away rather than suffer at the hands of Sarai.

However, Hagar's stance is much more subdued the second time around. In the E (Elohist) account, she has little self-fulfilling action. She is now a slave, and it is Sarah, also a mother, who controls her fate. Hagar must relish in her marginalized place. This mother finds herself and her teen son, Ishmael, ejected from the family compound. This is the matriarch's doing. Hagar is not haughty or arrogant. She is the epitome of a slave woman.[7]

The Hebrew word to describe Hagar is *shiphchah*. The word can mean "handmaid," "maidservant," or "slave girl." Each denotes that Hagar belongs to someone else and has the responsibility of meeting a superior's needs. As a slave girl, more specifically, she must render sexual and procreative functions to the male head of the household. Therefore, in this nineteenth-century BCE context, bearing a child for Abraham is just what Hagar the slave is supposed to do. Tammi Schneider, professor of the Old Testament, puts it this way:

6. John Waters, "Who Was Hagar," in *Stony the Road We Trod: African American Biblical Interpretation* (Minneapolis: Fortress Press, 1991), 192.
7. Ibid.

Hagar is defined as a *shiphchah* because it shows her status in the context of which she is living, highlights some of the functions she is intended to perform, and establishes the legitimacy of those around her to use her in that way. It does not mean that it is nice . . . but the references are to situate her rather than to demean her.[8]

The author avows, in essence, that Hagar's marginalized existence is just the way things were in that day and time.

Delores Williams's groundbreaking womanist approach to Hagar offers a similar take on her status. Williams purports that Hagar is a the maidservant of Sarai; yet she exercises much power. Bold enough to leave an abusive home, she puts herself and her unborn at risk as a runaway slave; however, she is bold enough to leave an abusive home. Additionally, Hagar names the place where she sees the Lord. No other female character in the biblical text does this.[9] Naming gives Hagar a semblance of significance. To name something also implies a degree of ownership. Hagar has been another's property; now she has the privilege of naming her own resource. She is no longer the object of possession, but she possesses something.

Williams argues that Hagar, as an Egyptian, would have been familiar with the god Ra, and her familiarity with Ra and the power associated with his eye is the religious backdrop for the naming encounter in the desert.[10] Thus, Hagar referring to "El-roi" as the "one who sees" is her way of recontextualizing her own Egyptian experiences with a "seeing" divinity. While it is the God of Abraham who rescues her, it is her African social location that provides a meeting of her master's god with her god. Hagar is out of Egypt, but Egyptian folkways and mores are not out of her.

This act of naming also speaks to the surrogacy roles Hagar fulfills.[11] She names a well associated with her "seeing" encounter with the Lord. This well would later serve as means of respite and refreshment for others. It is Hagar's responsibility to serve as nurse for any children born to Abram and Sarai. Her substituting for Sarai's role as mother is what causes her to be expelled and found wandering in the desert in the first place. Hagar is a human substitution and mediator on a physical,

8. Tammi J. Schneider, *Mothers of Promise: Women in the Book of Genesis* (Grand Rapids: Baker Books, 2008), 105.
9. Delores S. Williams, *Sisters in the Wilderness: The Challenge of Womanist God-Talk* (New York: Orbis Books, 1993), 23.
10. Ibid., 24.
11. Ibid., 22.

religious, familial, and maternal level. There is power notwithstanding her oppressed status as a slave.

Despite the surrogate roles, Hagar is economically disadvantaged. She does not have a permanent home. Her status as a slave finds her twice forced from her master's home through acts the mistress initiates. There are those who asseverate that Abraham acquires Hagar as a servant (J account), and she later becomes a slave (E narrative).[12] As Egyptians could hire themselves out to others, it is possible that Hagar initially volunteered to go with Abraham at some point during his sojourn to Egypt (Gen. 12:10). Either way, in the end, Hagar's class and rank vacillate. She moves from a servant in the household to homeless mother-slave.

As a homeless mother in a nomadic culture, Hagar and her son are at risk for violence and further exploitation. The desert is residence for both human and animal beasts. It is no place for a mother and her teen son. Hagar knows this and in desperation pleads for the Divine not to let her witness Ishmael's demise. Again a theophany, a visitation of God, her "El-Roi," saves the day.

Hagar does not remain homeless. She and Ishmael rebound from such dire straits. The biblical narrative is clear that divine intervention influences this mother's outcome. One cannot discount the inner drive and internal push that also compel Hagar to "keep it movin'." Whereas she totters between a house and homelessness, she does not remain without physical security. In the end, the Egyptian mother not only finds a roof for her and her son, but she also returns to Egypt, her homeland, to establish a nation. This once-homeless mother gives birth to that which would be the racial and ethnic home for many progeny. An Egyptian mother takes on the patriarchal role of Abraham when she finds a wife for her son, something prescribed for fathers in ancient Near Eastern families. Williams renders this summation: "Both Genesis 16 and 21 narratives reveal the faith, hope, and struggle with which an African slave woman worked through issues of survival, surrogacy, motherhood, rape, homelessness, and economic and sexual oppression."[13]

That was Hagar then. There are still "Hagars" and "Hagar's children" now.

---

12. Waters, "Who Was Hagar," 196.
13. Williams, *Sisters in the Wilderness*, 33.

HAGAR NOW

I have spent many years volunteering at a women's shelter. I take pleasure in participating in various worship services, disseminating toiletries
and clothes, playing with children, or just talking and listening to the
mothers for whom the shelter is their home and not some "community
service." The residents sometimes welcome my presence, at least that is
what I want to or need to believe.

The experience is also a source of pain for me. The reality is that
these mothers do not have a home to call their own. "Home" is a room
in a facility. "Home" is sharing a community bath, dining area and
kitchen. "Home" is depending on someone else for meals and wearing
clothes no one else wants. "Home" is children playing makeshift games
and seeking joy on a dilapidated playground. "Home" for the mothers and their children in a shelter is in essence being homeless. It is the
state of not having a home to call their own. Yet how dare I talk of pain
when I get to leave them and go to my home.

The plethora of exigencies that cause homelessness is as plentiful as
the mothers and children in the shelters. The loss of a job, a divorce,
a family disagreement, criminal activity, and just "life" are vicissitudes
that mothers today experience. They mirror Hagar and find themselves
in the desert pleading not to witness the death of their children. The
majority of mothers become homeless because of domestically violent
relationships. According to the National Coalition for the Homeless,
22 percent of mothers in shelters have had to choose between abuse
and the streets.[14] For so many their lives have been just as nomadic as
this biblical mother. More alarming is the fact that an overwhelming
majority of mothers in shelters are single. The parallels with Hagar are
palpable.

There is an economic dance between job security and homelessness. Mothers who make enough to secure food, clothing, and shelter
are less likely to find themselves in a shelter. The operative words are
"make enough." Women in general earn 77 cents for every dollar a
white man earns. African American women earn 64 cents. Women are
two-thirds of the minimum wage workers in positions that lack no paid
sick days.[15] For single mothers this means living in the fear and anxiety
that comes with sending a sick child to daycare or school.

14. National Coalition for the Homeless, http://www.nationalhomeless.org/factsheets/families.html.
15. The Shriver Report, *A Woman's Nation Pushes Back from the Brink: Facts and Figures*, http://shriverreport
.org/a-womans-nation-pushes-back-from-the-brink-facts-and-figures/.

This angst is compounded should a single mother lose a day's pay or perhaps a job. As some of the most established middle-class persons are a paycheck away from poverty, how much more urgent is the situation of a mother on paltry means who is the sole provider and caretaker. In 2013 the median weekly earnings for women twenty-five years old and older was $740 compared to $912 their male counterparts earned. African American women earned only $606.[16] African American women occupy 34 percent of professional and managerial positions compared to 43 percent of white women and 48 percent of Asian American women.[17] The class-race differential is just as profound in the twenty-first century as it was in Hagar's time. As race and class were factors in Hagar's story, they continue to reflect the socioeconomic status of African American mothers today.

If, as the National Coalition for the Homeless reports, 44 percent of the homeless have jobs, then one can only surmise how a person, a mother, can end up without a job.[18] Families with children now constitute 41 percent of the homeless population, and 42 percent of this population is African American. The composition of the average homeless family is a single-parent household headed by an African American female.[19] An astounding 72 percent of single-parent households are African American. This is not to make a sweeping statement that all families with just one parent are doing "poorly." Yet there are connections of race, class, and gender in certain compositions of African American families that reflect a perfect economic storm. The story of the African Hagar speaks volumes to African American mothers now. For too many, class status and lack of financial security make homelessness just a breath away.

It is heart wrenching to think of children who go to school from a shelter. Their address is that of an agency and not on a residential street or avenue. While we relish in being soccer, football, gymnastics, or other types of "moms," there are mothers who strive just to be the food, clothes, and shelter "mom." Sarah wanted to be a mother for the sake of cultural honor-shame. The mother in Hagar just wanted her son to live.

While the story of Hagar not only speaks to homelessness and choices,

16. Farah Ahmad, "How Women of Color Are Driving Entrepreneurship," Center for American Progress, https://www.americanprogress.org/issues/race/report/2014/06/10/91241/how-women-of-color-are-driving-entrepreneurship/.
17. Ibid.
18. National Coalition for the Homeless, http://www.nationalhomeless.org/factsheets/families.html.
19. Ibid.

it also rings of surrogacy. There are some women who choose not to or cannot bear children. Many seek alternative methods to fulfill their maternal calling. Although this is a new phenomenon among African American women, the idea of having a surrogate mother is becoming more accepted. All of the news surrounding in vitro fertilization and freezing eggs points to ways in which women are seeking alternative paths to motherhood. Wake Forest University professor and #NerdlandForever creator, Melissa Harris-Perry, and actress Sherri Shepherd are among the notable African American women countering narratives associated with the shame of barrenness.[20] *Being Mary Jane*, a television show about a successful broadcast reporter and her struggles to find love, has lifted discourse with a storyline of the lead character chronicling her fertility issues by freezing her eggs for future fertilization. In one episode she confiscated sperm of a lover, putting it in a baking soda container in the freezer.[21]

No one is affirming or advocating media portrayals and commentary regarding African American women and infertility. However, it is evident that African American women who long for motherhood, like Sarah, are exercising their options. Groups like Fertility for Colored Girls pool human and narrative resources to help African American women cope with issues related to infertility. Discussion topics include fibroid complications, miscarriages, and biological unknowns that may serve as medical roadblocks to motherhood.[22] African American women in and out of the spotlight are making decisions pertaining to the call of motherhood. Many are choosing to become mothers by other means.

The idea of surrogacy is not a new one among African American women. As discussed in chapter 1, history is replete with stories showing how women took care of one another's children. From the role of mammy to othermothering and communal mothering, African American mothers have had to care for those who did not come through their womb. The concept of neighborhood mothering and communal mothering as surrogacy is a part of the landscape among African American female relationships. The antebellum and postbellum periods reflect the nature of such surrogacy.

20. Melissa Harris-Perry, "The Surrogacy Journey She Took for Her Daughter," *The Huffington Post*, http://www.huffingtonpost.com/2014/02/18/melissa-harris-perry-baby-surrogacy-ivf_n_4808049.html. "Inside Sherri Shepherd's Surrogacy Baby Drama," *People*, http://www.people.com/article/sherri-shepherd-custody-battle-baby-surrogate-divorce-lamar-sally-interview.

21. "Storm Advisory," *Being Mary Jane*, episode no. 1, first broadcast January 7, 2014, by Black Entertainment Television, directed by Salim Akil and written by Jessica Mecklenburg.

22. Fertility for Colored Girls, http://www.fertilityforcoloredgirls.org/#!projects/c21kz.

The antebellum era speaks to forced surrogacy. The female slave has no say in giving birth to and caring for the slave master's child. The former she did on her own time. The latter was at the mistress's beck and call. Williams notes, ". . . it was often the mammy who taught and instilled values in white children . . . . Mammies acted as protectors of their young white charges."[23] Like the slave system in the days of Abraham and Sarah, slavery in the United States demanded that slave women surrender their bodies, like Hagar.[24]

However, after the Emancipation Proclamation and during Reconstruction, economics still forced black woman to pursue surrogacy as a job. Many took to working in white homes and caring for white children to make ends meet. The sexual dynamics were a little different. Black women were not forced into sexual relationships with white bosses. However, it was not uncommon to hear of some men forcing themselves on their black help.[25] Black women could refuse now that slavery had ended.

Williams adds this final analysis on the current state of surrogacy:

> Today the growing surrogacy industry in North American and the escalating poverty . . . can pressure poor black women to become heavily involved in this industry at the level of reproduction . . . the point here is that since emancipation, black women have been able to exercise choice with regard to surrogacy roles.[26]

Although Sarah forced Hagar to become a mother for her, the sisterhood of surrogacy did not maintain an oppressive theme. Now surrogacy represents a type of economic self-determination for African American women wanting to help other women become mothers. This is "Hagar revisited."[27]

CONCLUSION

Through motherhood, the story of Hagar reminds the reader to consider the dynamics between the oppressed and oppressor. One woman's desire to be a mother has ripple effects for another woman under her authority. This mother-to-mother interaction exposes one degree

---

23. Williams, *Sisters in the Wilderness*, 62.
24. Ibid., 71.
25. Ibid., 72.
26. Ibid., 61.
27. Ibid., 83.

of gender positioning. The fact that Hagar has to yield her body to the patriarch, Abraham, demonstrates another side of the gender coin. Class is the key factor that perpetuates displacement and homelessness for a mother, Hagar. Sarah remains secure in her husband's house while Hagar and the same husband's seed must dwell in the desert.

The biblical text does not shy away from highlighting Hagar's race as an Egyptian. As an African she is able to recontextualize her master and mistress's god through her own religious lens. Although Hagar is marginalized, her role as a social, familial, and maternal surrogate speak to her own authority and wherewithal. It is this same personal force that this mother uses to struggle through homelessness and to survive in order to find a home for her son and generations to come. Hagar goes home to Egypt to establish a home for others who would come through her. This story is a case of womanist maternal thought, because it addresses motherhood through race, class, and gender. And in the end, this mother is homeless no more.

Questions for Discussion

1. Which story of Hagar, Sarah, and Abraham most appeals to you: Genesis 16 or Genesis 21? Why?
2. What is your reaction to the Lord sending Hagar back to her owners?
3. What does it mean to be homeless? What have you done for the homeless?
4. Is there a shame associated with bearing a child for someone else? Is there shame in not being able to bear children?
5. What is this lesson teaching you to do and to be?

5

Rizpah: A Childless Mother

2 Samuel 21:1–14

Sometimes I feel like a childless mother, Sometimes I feel like a
   childless mother,
Sometimes I feel like a childless mother, A long way from home . . . .
                             —Stephanie Buckhanon Crowder
(Sung to the tune of "Sometimes I Feel Like a Motherless Child")

What an event this was going to be. It was the hottest ticket in town.
Mothers from across the United States would descend on the sandy
beaches of Weston, Florida. There was the promise of good weather,
good food, and the joy of mother-sisterhood. It would be a time of
laughter, dancing, talking, crying, and healing. The Circle of Mothers
Empowerment Retreat was definitely the place for any mother to be.
That is, if you were the mother of homicide victim.

Sybrina Fulton, the mother of Trayvon Martin, established the
Trayvon Martin Foundation in honor of her teenage son who was
gunned down while carrying Skittles and a can of tea. The Foundation
spearheaded the Circle of Mothers Empowerment Retreat in response
to the number of mothers trying to make sense out of senseless acts of
violence perpetrated on their children. Keynote speaker Afeni Shakur
headlined the event. It had been over a decade since bullets silenced the
rapping voice of her son, Tupac.

Add Lucia McBath and Lesley McSpadden to this strange circle.
Their sons were also shot to death. Jordan Davis, McBath's child, was
killed in a gas station over a dispute involving loud music.[1] McSpadden watched her son's (Michael Brown) dead body lie near his apart-
ment complex for four to six hours after a police officer killed him for

---

1. The documentary *3 ½ Minutes* recounts the murder of Jordan Davis in a parking lot in November 2012. See
Ryan Buxton, "Jordan Davis' Parents Open Up about Coping with Their Son's Death and the Documentary "3 ½
Minutes," *Huffpost Black Voices*, January 30, 2015, http://www.huffingtonpost.com/2015/01/30/jordan-davis-3
-12-minutes_n_6581934.html.

"walking in the street."[2] Between the murders of Davis and Brown, news of Freddie Gray's death arose. Somehow he suffered a broken spine while in police custody. His mother, Gloria Darden, also knows about public grief due to a child's murder.[3] Little is known of the whereabouts of LaQuan McDonald's mother. Yet the sixteen shots that riveted his body and the subsequent police cover-up is enough for any mother to mourn in her stead.[4] The list grows.

From these mothers to the mother next door to mothers of slavery and the Middle Passage, history is heavy with their maternal moans and mourning. The blood and bodies of their sons and daughters pervade the earth. Although a bullet, a beating, a gun, or a gang has taken their children, these mothers are still . . . mothers. They are childless mothers who perpetually must wrestle with the monstrous hollowness only the loss of a child can produce. For the rest of their lives these mothers must live with death.

The biblical record gives insight into what it means to be a childless mother. The oft-overlooked story of Rizpah in 2 Samuel is a horrific glimpse of the agony and pain a mother endures when her children are killed. Rizpah's account highlights her efforts to protect and secure her children, her dead children. Like the aforementioned women, she shows the reader how mothers learn to literally dwell in death.

TEXT SUMMARY

(2 Samuel 21:1–14)

Second Samuel 21:1–14 records the narrative of Rizpah and the death of her children. This story begins with David still finding his way as the new king. After having endured family drama, he now faces a famine. Israel has been without food for three years. After this third year of nothing to eat, David asks the Lord, "What's going on?"

The Lord tells David that famine is in the land because of the Gibeonites. Saul, David's predecessor, mistreated them because he felt they were racially inferior to him; the land is cursed because of

2. Michael Brown was shot six times on August 9, 2014. See "What Happened in Ferfuson," *New York Times*, updated August 10, 2015, http://www.nytimes.com/interactive/2014/08/13/us/ferguson-missouri-town -under-siege-after-police-shooting.html?_r=0.

3. Melanie Eversley, "Freddie Grey's Mother Attempts Suicide," *USA Today*, October 23, 2015, http://www .usatoday.com/story/news/2015/10/22/report-freddie-gray-mother-attempts-suicide/74423300/.

4. Dean Reynolds, "The Brief, Troubled Life of Laquan McDonald, *CBS Evening News*, December 12, 2015, http://www.cbsnews.com/news/the-brief-troubled-life-of-laquan-mcdonald/.

his misbehavior. Gibeonites were descendants of the Canaanites—the
people who dwelt in the land promised to Abraham's progeny. Ironically, Saul had given his word that he would not harm the Gibeonites.
Reneging on his promise, he decided to kill them anyway. David, his
people, and the land were reaping what Saul had sown. It is called
systemic decay. Such a demise occurs when the immoral actions of the
political leaders cause harm to people under their rule. The oppressed
suffer because of the hard, heavy hand of the oppressor. The nation
suffers due to the personal indiscretions of its leader.

David summons the Gibeonites and asks them twice about how
to rectify the matter. Instead of gold or silver, they wanted blood for
blood to ameliorate the situation. As Saul had slaughtered their own,
they wanted to slaughter Saul's—a body for a body for justice. Since
Saul is dead, the Gibeonites argue that any of his children will do.
David decides that seven of Saul's descendants will die. He gives five
of Saul's grandsons to the Gibeonites in addition to the sons of Saul's
concubine, Rizpah. He withholds the child of Saul's son Jonathan.

The Gibeonites impale and hang all seven men, leaving their decomposing bodies in the open for months, during which time Rizpah, day
in and day out, covers the remains. She protects not only her dead
sons, but those belonging to Saul's oldest daughter, Merab. The text
declares that David learns of Rizpah's motherly yet peculiar act. Seeing this mother's devotion to the dead, the king realizes that he has
some unfinished business with dead bodies. David retrieves the unbur-
ied bodies of Saul and Jonathan that were with the Philistines. Using
a tomb belonging to Saul's father, Kish, David buries all nine bodies:
Saul and Jonathan, the five sons of Merab, and the two sons of Rizpah.
At this point, the famine lifts from Israel.

RIZPAH THEN

Rizpah was not the wife. She was the concubine, the "side piece," if you
will. Concubines in the eleventh century BCE were basically women
who provided sexual pleasures to their owner or anyone who lorded
over them.[5] The concubine did not have the privileges of a wife. Any
children born to that union had no patrilineal standing. In essence, the
concubine's only value was her body. The children were worth even

---

5. "Concubine," Bible Hub, http://biblehub.com/topical/c/concubine.htm.

less. Thus, by Rizpah's social status alone, there was little she could do about her or her children's well-being.

Biblical scholar Cheryl Exum disagrees with classifying Rizpah as a concubine. She maintains the English translation (cf. 2 Sam 3:7 NRSV and others) is misleading. The Hebrew term for concubine, *pilegesh*, pronounced "pee-leh'-ghesh," can refer to a wife of secondary status and not just an unmarried paramour.[6] Thus Rizpah is a widow of the former king and connected to the dynasty that preceded David.

Exum says "wife." I aver "concubine." Regardless, Rizpah lacks power. First, even if she were Saul's wife, he is now dead. Therefore, as a widow of the past king, she would have no royal power. Second, the new king, who is not Rizpah's husband or lover, uses his power to decide the fate of her children. In either case she is without royal agency and social authority. Her maternal capacity is another matter.

The story with David and the Gibeonites is not the first time Rizpah is the pawn of sexist, political games. She initially comes on the scene in 2 Samuel 3 when Ish-bosheth, or Ishbaal, Saul's son, is outraged that one of King Saul's enemies has a sexual encounter with his concubine, Rizpah. To have such a relationship with the king's property was a sign of disrespect. Any move of this sort incited rebellion. It is ironic that a concubine with little social clout could be the root cause of national warfare. Rizpah had no power, but yet she was powerful.

This class dynamic resurfaces when Rizpah serves as political fodder during the reign of David. To appease the Gibeonites, David offers the sons of a concubine. David is the king. Rizpah is subject to the king's authority. He could do with her and her seed whatever he wanted, even to the point of death. David is aware of this class dynamic and acts accordingly.

Class is also at play as Rizpah exposes her body to nature's elements for at least six months ensuring that no vultures eat the seven decomposing bodies. This mother not only risks her life for her children, but she does so for the sake of boys that are not her own. The Bible does not record Merab, the former king's daughter, exposing herself to the elements to make any attempt to cover her own. Although both mothers must reckon with imperial homicide, the daughter of the king does not "get off her high horse" to protest the injustice. Yet she too is a victim, even in her royal state. She does not have say over her own children. King David controls her sons as well.

6. J. Cheryl Exum, "Rizpah," *Word and World* 17 (1997): 261.

Merab experiences further exploitation in a literary sense because the text records not the names of Merab's five sons but the names of Rizpah's two children. One of Rizpah's sons is named Mephibosheth. He shares the same name as Saul's grandson, a child born to his son Jonathan. Yet one with the name lives, the other dies. The class conundrum is compelling.

As there are glaring implications for class in the text, gender dynamics are just as palpable. David does not offer Jonathan's son, Mephibosheth, to the Gibeonites. Yet he finds five other grandsons and two sons who are Jonathan's relatives. The common denominator here is that the five grandsons and sons belong to women who perchance are not dear to David. They, like Mephibosheth, are potential claimants to the Saulide throne, since Saul's three eldest sons died at Mount Gilboa (1 Sam. 31). Thus one could surmise that David uses the famine to justify getting rid of any threat to his kingdom.[7]

The seven sons are expendable, and more so because of their connection to the women in Saul's life. David and Jonathan shared an intimate friendship (1 Sam. 18). Although Saul offers his daughter, Merab's hand in marriage, David decides that he is not good enough for her (1 Sam. 18). There is no further biblical commentary on the two. Just as mute is any word on Rizpah and David. As far as the reader is concerned, their presence in 2 Samuel 21 is the first time the narrator notes them in tandem.

Rizpah's lack of authority is more apparent through her silence. David and the Gibeonites handle the negotiating. The men do all of the talking. They discuss what will become of the mothers' children. No record describes Rizpah or Merab as getting the opportunity to have their say or object to the proceedings; they are voiceless figures who must let the men run the show. Merab becomes voiceless and invisible, as there is no record of her saying or doing anything in response to David's edict. Rizpah can only speak with her body as it protects her sons from the elements. Exum purports: "Silence gives Rizpah a preternatural magnitude and underscores the gravity of the ritual she performs."[8] Her body language is the only communication allowed.

Nonetheless, Rizpah's long and solitary vigil outwardly dramatizes her private loss in a public action that commands David's attention. Her labor of love and death prevents David and his people from perishing.

7. Valerie Bridgeman, "The Inspiration of Rizpah's Courageous Helplessness," in *Global Perspectives on the Bible*, ed. Mark Roncace and Joseph Weaver (Boston: Pearson Education, 2014), 105.
8. Cheryl Exum, "Rizpah," in *Women in Scripture*, ed. Carol Myers (Grand Rapids: Eerdmans, 2000), 145.

Through the season, she cares for the dead because men with power do not care for the living.[9] She engages in necro-care day and night unceasingly. As her sons and Saul's five grandsons are human sacrifices to right a political wrong, so is Rizpah a maternal sacrifice. She has little social agency or royal authority, but her mother power is sagacious.

The connections between caring for the land and caring for the body are glaring. Israel suffers a drought, and God tells David that someone must right a national wrong. The Gibeonites want bodies to help rectify the curse in the land. Rizpah cares for the bodies of the sons during the harvest season until the rain falls. Once David buries all of the men, the land is free to produce and yield.

Although David and Rizpah had not been in relationship, they are as joined as the land is to the body politics. Their connection is so intertwined that "Rizpah is responsible not only for the resolution to the dishonor suffered by Saul's house but also . . . for the divine receptivity to human supplication that brings the story (of Saul) to closure."[10] In the end, a voiceless woman does what a negotiating man could do not for his own kingdom.

RIZPAH NOW

Rizpah cares for another woman's dead children. She put herself in harm's way to hover over the bodies of children who are in a class above hers. While taking care of her dead sons, she also takes care of the dead sons of royalty. Death does not erase motherhood. A mother is always a mother.

The parallels to African American mothers tending to the progeny of a master or overseer or anyone beyond their class are resounding. As African mothers developed a network of othermothering or communal mothering to share the responsibilities of caring for children, they recontextualized this idea during slavery in the slave-mistress-master triad. Nursing the slave owners' children was part of the female slave's duty. As previously noted, even during Reconstruction, women of African heritage were still "the help" and the face of domestic work and motherly care. This is maternal obligation wrapped in class expectation.

African American mothers know how to deal with death. Society

9. Ibid.
10. Gerald West, "1 and 2 Samuel," in *Global Bible Commentary*, Daniel Patte, ed. (Nashville: Abingdon Press, 2004), 103.

forces African American mothers to learn how to deal with death. The
number of children "impaled" (2 Sam. 21:9) due to gang violence,
police abuse, bad drug deals, and being in the crossfire is appalling. As
the seven bodies of Rizpah and Merab's children are on public display,
the bullet-ridden body of a dead Michael Brown laid on the street of
Ferguson, Missouri, for over four hours. There are Rizpahs today as
there were over three thousand years ago.

Additionally, African American mothers deal with the political
powers that perpetuate demise. For Rizpah and Merab, it was political
warfare. The political warfare today is a different sort. Inequalities in
sentencing, the failure to press criminal charges of certain groups, the
presence of juries lacking people of color, and the acquittal of defen-
dants representing specific racial and class backgrounds are all a part of
today's political and judicial warfare.

African American mothers know the bloodshed and death such
battles produce. In the same vein, death is death. Instead of heart disease and cancer, the leading cause of death for African American males
ages fifteen to forty-four is homicide.[11] The stat became more telling
as the country publicly wrestled with the back-to-back deaths of Trayvon Martin, Jordan Davis, Michael Brown, Renisha McBride, Tanisha
Anderson, Eric Gardner, and so many other black people. The images
of their African American mothers weeping profusely continues to fill
the airwaves as they deal with death with the world watching. Countless other mothers must weep in silence, out of the public view. They,
too, give their lives to secure their children, even unto death.

Like Rizpah these mothers face class challenges. A number of the
African American males killed come from single-parent homes where
mothers are struggling to make ends meet. This is not to generalize
that households with only a mother or a father experience homicide.
Referring again to Patricia Collins: "As the testimonies of numerous
African-Americans raised by their mothers suggest, such families are
not inherently a problem. Rather the alarming trend is the persistent poverty of African-American women and children living in such
households."[12]

Too many narratives of African American male victims include elements of their living in environments where survival is the order of the
day. Studies show that when society adds poverty and economics issues

11. The Center of Disease Control and Prevention, *Leading Causes of Death by Age Group, Black Males-United States, 2010*, http://www.cdc.gov/men/lcod/2010/LCODBlackmales2010.pdf.
12. Collins, *Black Feminist Thought*, 63.

to the forefront, there can be life.[13] Lack of financial stability, job security, and the fiscal means to buy food, clothing, and shelter are a class death sentence.

Additionally, "death" for African American mothers does not always mean hovering over a corpse. The level of punishment African American children experience in school can lead to a different type of "death." The Department of Education reports that black and brown children get harsher school discipline than their white counterparts.[14] African American children are three times more likely to get suspended or expelled for acts that would warrant children of other racial and ethnic groups a slap on the wrist.[15] These suspensions cause children to miss class time and get behind in coursework. Such can easily lead to failing classes and students dropping out of school. The job market does not look too kindly on anyone without a high school diploma; for many, criminal activity becomes a source of income and survival. Without proper advocacy or a "Rizpah" to intervene, this pathway puts African American children and their mothers on the road to social death.

The number of African American males in prison is another form of death. African American males are 6 percent of the U.S. population and 40 percent of those incarcerated.[16] One in three young African American men is under the jurisdiction of the criminal justice system. African Americans constitute 15 percent of drug users in the United States and 90 percent of those incarcerated for drug-related charges.[17] African American men have been imprisoned more than thirteen times the rate of white men.[18] So death does not always mean the absence of breath, but it can also be actions or conditions that are not life-giving or life-affirming. Nonetheless, these can make for a slow death.

Like Rizpah, mothers "watch over" and visit sons, husbands, cousins, and nephews in jail who are dying a slow social, economic, and moral death. Many will die a prison death as they face capital punishment or life without parole. For the men released, many still do not have a chance to live. Laws make it difficult if not impossible for felons

13. Emily Badger, "Chicago Gave Hundreds of High-Risk Kids a Summer Job. Violent Crime Arrests Plummeted," *The Washington Post*, December 26, 2014, http://www.washingtonpost.com/blogs/wonkblog/wp/2014/12/26/chicago-gave-hundreds-of-high-risk-kids-a-summer-job-violent-crime-arrests-plummeted/.
14. U.S. Department of Education Office for Civil Rights, "Civil Rights Data Collection: Data Snapshot: School Discipline," http://www2.ed.gov/about/offices/list/ocr/docs/crdc-discipline-snapshot.pdf.
15. U.S. Department of Education Office for Civil Rights, "Civil Rights Data Collection: Data Snapshot: School Discipline," http://www2.ed.gov/about/offices/list/ocr/docs/crdc-discipline-snapshot.pdf.
16. Alexander, *The New Jim Crow*, 59.
17. Ibid., 103.
18. Ibid., 98.

to vote, get federal aid, find employment, or join the military. Yet we wonder why recidivism is so great.

"Rizpahs" today face death. It is not because they and their children are fodder in kingdom games. African American mothers walking in the shoes of Rizpah today must guard children caught in the crossfire of unjust laws, vigilante neighbors, gangs, and unequal school discipline.

What happens when mothers cause themselves to be childless? Women sometimes bring about their child's demise. African American women have abortions. Sometimes mothers decide they do not want to be mothers any more. It is not a topic people like to address. The idea is not to judge anyone but to remember that not all women want to be mothers. Just as there are African American women who long to be mothers, there are African American mothers who do not and have taken medical steps to not be a mother. An African-American woman is almost five times likelier to have an abortion than a white woman, and a Latina more than twice as likely, according to the Centers of Disease Control and Prevention.[19] At almost every income level, African Americans have higher unintended pregnancy and abortion rates than whites or Latinas. In an article from *The Atlantic,* Bracey Sherman observes, "There's a very unfortunate stereotype of women of color, and black women in particular, that we are promiscuous and just have babies. You don't want that to be you."[20]

Zoie Dutton's article implies that one cause of black women and women of color having abortions is to not be seen as sexually loose or characterized as a "baby momma." Of course the pro-choice respondents may argue whether the fetus is a child or just a seed or some strange-looking mass. My point is not to argue pro or con. Women should have the right to choose what they do with their bodies, not men, especially those in legislative positions. The purpose for the sake of this work is to state that some African American women make decisions regarding motherhood that do not always end with a baby shower and cute little baby clothes.

Other conditions contribute to mothers precipitation into childlessness. Exposing children to smoking, drug abuse, alcoholic behavior, and domestic violence can do them harm and lead to their demise, causing the mother to become a childless mother. Secondhand cigarette

19. Centers for Disease Control and Prevention, "Abortion Surveilence, 2006," http://www.cdc.gov/mmwr/preview/mmwrhtml/ss5808a1.htm?s_cid=ss5808a1_e.

20. Zoie Dutton, "Abortion's Racial Gap," *The Atlantic,* http://www.theatlantic.com/health/archive/2014/09/abortions-racial-gap/380251/.

and blunt smoke causes asthma and other respiratory problems. Drugs impact parental behavior and judgment that can endanger children. Children of alcoholic parents and victims of domestic violence become vulnerable to life-threatening circumstances. The sheer exposure to such erratic adult behavior can change a child's own way of thinking and behaviors toward others and him or herself. The National Association for Children of Alcoholics notes,

> Children of addicted parents are the highest risk group of children to become alcohol and drug abusers due to both genetic and family environment factors. . . . Addicted parents often lack the ability to provide structure or discipline in family life, but simultaneously expect their children to be competent at a wide variety of tasks earlier than do non-substance-abusing parents. . . . Most welfare professionals (79.6%) report that substance abuse causes or contributes to at least half of all cases of child maltreatment; 39.7% say it is a factor in over 75% of the cases.[21]

The Rizpah factor displays itself in sundry ways. Just as a king determined the fate of this biblical mother, current-day political structures can dictate the livelihood of African American women and their children. These mothers face many challenges that give rise to their watching over the bodies of their deceased sons and daughters.

CONCLUSION

Sybrina Fulton, Lesley McSpadden, Gloria Darden, and Lucia McBath represent modern-day Rizpahs. They are mothers who know what it is like to have a child killed. They are familiar with the impotence that comes when your child's life is literally taken from you, taken from this world. The perpetrator who killed Fulton's son got away with the crime. The man who shot McBath's son is now behind bars. No charges were pressed against the cop who killed McSpadden's child. These three mothers have not been silent. Their voices and pleas for justice are stentorian.

Like Rizpah, Fulton, McBath, McSpadden, and so many others are changing the national landscape. The perpetual action, the constant heralding, the incessant pleas for justice continue to go forth despite

21. National Association for Children of Alcoholics, http://www.nacoa.net/pdfs/addicted.pdf.

what appears to be a drought in righteousness and morality. However, if there is any merit in the story of this concubine, it is that society can't discount a mother's love, no matter how peculiar, odd, or strange it may be. A mother's pain has the potential to change the world.

Questions for Discussion

1. Discuss your initial reactions to the story of Rizpah.
2. Explain if a mother can ever be "childless."
3. What is causing "death" in the world today?
4. What are you willing to do for "dead" people in "dead" situations today?
5. What action can you take that could help change the landscape of this nation?

6

Bathsheba: A Fearless Mother

1 Kings 1:11–31

I didn't know my own strength,
and I crashed down and I tumbled,
but I did not crumble . . .
     —Sung by Whitney Houston (Lyrics by Diane Warren)[1]

We are prone to remember the bad rather than the good. We love to swim in the cesspool of personal tragedy, bad behavior, or a fall from grace. If people redeem themselves or recover from some scandal, society will forgive for a moment. However, the mental recall of moral turpitude is for a lifetime. There is a tendency to disrobe a person's present condition and reveal the nakedness of what she used to be, what he used to do.

The story of the late pop icon Whitney Houston is one such example. All of the Grammys, American Music Awards, and BET Honors point minimally to her talent. The magic of her voice cannot be captured in music awards. Houston's vocal range in her early years could take the simplest lyrics and turn them into something vocally indescribable. Remember her rendition of "The Star Spangled Banner"? Iconic! Epic!

Yet the images of coroners taking her dead body away tend to overshadow Houston's lyrical legacy. Reports of a drug overdose throw shade on any musical light Houston shined. Sure, no one can forget her last attempt to sing her way back into the spotlight. The honesty of "I Didn't Know My Own Strength" allowed us to join in her confession. Death, drugs, and demise in a hotel bathroom forced us to wrestle

---

1. Whitney Houston, "I Didn't Know My Own Strength" by Diane Warren on *I Look to You*, Arista Records, 2009, CD recording.

with Houston's weakness. The world will not forget the soaring sounds of Houston. The world will more readily remember what silenced her.

In examining the story of Bathsheba as a fearless mother, there is bad-woman-good-matriarch-bad-woman tension. Ask anyone who Bathsheba was, and the most immediate answer: "She is the woman, bathing on the roof, who slept with David." Rarely will anyone note Bathsheba's role in securing the kingdom for her son, Solomon. Even if readers mention this, they revert back to the "woman who caused David to kill her husband Uriah." Society likes a good story but loves the bad stuff. This chapter seeks to move Bathsheba from an eroticized, voiceless object to a savvy, articulate matriarch.

TEXT SUMMARY

(1 Kings 1:11–31)

First Kings paints a different picture of Bathsheba from the one introduced in 2 Samuel. Bathsheba first comes on the biblical scene as capturing King David's attention during her afternoon bath (2 Sam. 11). David inquires about her, sleeps with her, and kills her husband, Uriah. Then David marries Bathsheba. She conceives and bears a son. God punishes them by not allowing their child to live. Almost immediately there is a second pregnancy. Solomon is born.

There is no further word on either Bathsheba or Solomon until over two decades later. At this stage David is physically fragile and on his deathbed (1 Kgs. 1). The date is circa 967 BCE. Solomon's older half-brother, Adonijah, has proclaimed himself king. Nathan, the prophet, feels disregarded and more so afraid. He quickly tells Bathsheba that her son's stake in the Davidic throne is in jeopardy. He reminds Bathsheba that David promised the kingdom to Solomon, and unless she acts quickly, she and her son will die.

Bathsheba pays obeisance to the ailing king, her husband, and informs him of the older son's dealings. Adding to the recommended discourse given by Nathan, the queen declares to David: "But you, my lord the king—the eyes of all Israel are on you to tell them who shall sit on the throne of my lord the king after him (1:20). Nathan enters to cosign on Bathsheba's story and to confirm Adonijah's royal coup.

David summons Bathsheba back to his bedside and assures her that everything will be alright. Solomon will be large and in charge. In one of his last acts, as potentate the king puts matters in motion and declares

Solomon his successor. Adonijah hears of this and quickly ceases and desists his feeble efforts at the crown.

Bathsheba's prowess rises to the surface once again in 1 Kings 2. After David's death, Adonijah goes to Bathsheba requesting the king's caretaker, Abishag. The queen mother goes to her son, King Solomon, and intercedes for her half-son, Adonijah. Solomon, although promising to give his mother whatever she wants, does not grant Adonijah the care of Abishag. For him, the request itself is a royal threat. In the end the king-brother slays his half-brother and his cohorts. There is no further commentary on Bathsheba.

BATHSHEBA THEN

The Bathsheba of 1 Kings is not the Bathsheba of 2 Samuel. Yes, they are the same in name, but the Bathsheba in 1 King is "a grown woman." She comes on the scene as a silent royal subject; then she develops into a wise, cunning figure. She has seen some of the bloodshed in her husband's kingdom. Knowing that her son Solomon is not at the head of the heir-to-the-throne line, Bathsheba raises her voice and acts. She leads her own palace coup to squash the coup of another mother's child, a mother who also bore a son to her husband, the king. In the end, Solomon would be the only one of David's seventeen sons to reign.[2]

Whereas Bathsheba's entrance onto the biblical scene is as a sexualized woman, now the narrative involving her has little erotic connotation. Although Bathsheba attends to many of David's physical needs, he is old and needs young Abishag to warm him. The text is clear that she is not a concubine; they do not have sexual intercourse. Hence, a contrast between Abishag and Bathsheba. The class differential is intriguing. The queen does not have time to be a blanket for the king.

Bathsheba in 1 Kings 1–2 is politically savvy. She plays a man's game in a patriarchal world. The gender nuances manifest. A woman at the urging of a man bows and speaks to another man on behalf of a third man. Bathsheba's verbal strategy and acumen force the hand of the main man to save not only her but also other men. Because the actions center around Bathsheba's intervention, one could argue that

---

2. Mignon Jacobs, "Mothering a Leader: Bathsheba's Relational and Functional Identities," in *Mother Goose, Mother Jones, Mommie Dearest: Biblical Mothers and Their Children* ed. Cheryl A. Kirk-Duggan and Tina Pippin (Atlanta: Society of Biblical Literature, 2009), 72.

she is still domestically and sexually liberated. She is not who she used to be. She has come a long way. She is not voiceless. The queen, and soon to be queen mother, is poised and calculating in what she says and what she does.[3]

Bathsheba's rhetorical prowess pushes King David to act. Unlike her first encounter with David, Bathsheba's words, not her body, appeal to him. She initiates conversation with a title, "My lord." She embellishes Nathan's words and declares that David "swore to the LORD your God," so that his promise is not just to her but an oath to God. Therefore, Bathsheba quotes and does not paraphrase David. This is a promise of the historical present. As God had promised that there would always be a seed of David on the throne, and now that David is about to die, Bathsheba helps to usher this fulfillment. Finally, she reiterates her husband's promise that Solomon would reign in the future so that it contrasts with her description of Adonijah reigning in the present.

The relationship between Bathsheba and Nathan is peculiar. It is apparent that Nathan is trying to save himself. In this male-centered, male-dominated world, he goes to a woman for refuge. Ironically, this is the same Nathan who in 1 Samuel chastised David and Bathsheba about their illicit affair. Now he needs her protection. Granny always said, "The same people you mistreat going up, you will need on your way down." Nevertheless, Bathsheba plots with Nathan and bedecks what he tells her to say. Again, Bathsheba is not the young girl she was twenty years prior. She tells King David that his people, Israel, are expecting him to do something. "You are old, but you are not dead, yet!" Old Testament professor Mignon Jacobs argues, "After laying out the information, Bathsheba defines the situation with respect to the nation, thus taking the focus off herself and appearing to be concerned about David's reputation and national status."[4] Bathsheba reminds David that what he is about to do is bigger than he is. This is nation work, and her son Solomon will continue his legacy.

After all of her bowing, she ultimately calls David's royal bluff. This is a fearless woman. Her life is on the line. Her son's future is at stake. She has been silent, but it is evident she has been watching her husband the king and other men play with their political toys. The class dynamic here is compelling. A subject of the king forces the king's royal hand.

A point of discrepancy is that there is no biblical account of David

---

3. Kristine Garroway, "Was Bathsheba the Original Bridget Jones?", *Nashim: Journal of Jewish Women's Studies* 24 (2013): 61.

4. Jacobs, *Mother Goose*, 79.

making any promise to Solomon. God tells David that someone will build the temple (2 Sam. 7:12–16). The text does not mention Solomon or any of David's sons by name. The verbiage Nathan gives to Bathsheba and Bathsheba to David about Solomon is undocumented in the Bible. The biblical editing in this succession narrative is a stroke of genius. The editor crafts history anew for the sake of royalty and legacy. Yet it is a woman orchestrating such matters in a patriarchal world. As succession stories construct the who, how, and when of the kingdom, the dialogue between Nathan, Bathsheba, and David epitomizes this literary genre.

As Bathsheba intervenes and handles a national crisis, she secures the future of her son. She is no longer the object of male desire but displays finesse in playing a man's game. If this were a game of spades, one would say she was trump tight. Bathsheba is not naked on a roof but clothed and in her right mind and using the right words. Her verbal game and regal strategy get her what she wants. She knows what to say to stroke the man's ego, even a dying man's ego. True, she is still a pawn in patriarchy in that Nathan knew how to incite her. It is just as correct that before David makes a move, he guarantees Bathsheba that both and she and Solomon will fare well.

As queen mother, Bathsheba goes to great lengths to safeguard the newly minted King Solomon. The ousted Adonijah does not just leave the premises: he dares to make a request. Instead of going to his half-brother, he goes to the queen mother for a favor. To ask for the king's concubine was a slap in the royal face. Abishag was not David's concubine, but her role of providing for him could be perceived as intimate, although nonsexual. It is likely that Bathsheba's years as one of King David's wives alerted her to the power dynamic surrounding the king's concubine, and in this case, the king's "bed warmer."

Bathsheba does not innocently take Adonijah's request to her son, King Solomon. As a model mother-leader, Bathsheba is a skillful negotiator in the family-public domain.[5] She knows and clearly calculates the nature of the petition. True to regal form, Solomon expunges not only Adonijah but all who are associated with his initial attempt to overtake the throne. Once more, a woman is at the heart of the machinations of men. All hail, the queen mother, Bathsheba, the fearless one!

5. Ibid., 82.

BATHSHEBA NOW

People can say what they will about Whitney Houston, but she knew what she had and used it accordingly. She had a gift. Drug addiction did not allow her to care for the gift as she should have, but her voice was special nonetheless. Although the executives at Arista capitalized on her talents, she knew how to make money for herself and in the end for her daughter, Bobbi Kristina Brown. It is striking that her ex-husband did not get any material goods or money from the divorce proceedings. In her will, she left everything to her only child. She had her struggles, but there were points of future and financial lucidity. Her daughter's security seemed to be integral to her. Bobbi Kristina was financially secure even to her untimely death.[6]

Like Houston, there are many African American mothers for whom "this is business." Akin to Bathsheba they have learned the moves and methods to thriving in a man's world. I would posit that security for themselves and their family has been a driving force. The Center for American Progress reports that African American women-owned businesses grew by 258 percent from 1997 to 2013, reflecting a total of 1.1 million such enterprises.[7] African American women are starting businesses at a rate six times the national average.[8] They own 16 percent of the businesses that women have started in the past eighteen years.[9] Many partially funded their enterprises themselves. Credit cards, savings, family, friends, and business lines of credit help to take up the venture capital slack. Lack of fair pay, fair promotions, and family-friendly policies spur such entrepreneurship among African American women.[10] Yet, as Farah Ahmad notes, these owners of beauty shops, comedy clubs, restaurants, and daycares are finding ways to make their dreams of entrepreneurship come true.[11]

However, African American women, mothers in particular, have not found success on Wall Street. For example, the world of the Fortune 500 is indeed a white world, and it is also a man's world. More than

---

6. Bobbi Kristina died July 26, 2015, after being found unconscious in a bathtub in January 2015. The consequences surrounding her death are surreal in that it rings of her mother's death in 2012. http://www.cbsnews.com/news/bobbi-kristina-brown-dead-at-22/.

7. Farah Ahmad, "How Women of Color Are Driving Entrepreneurship," The Center for American Progress, https://www.americanprogress.org/issues/race/report/2014/06/10/91241/how-women-of-color-are-driving-entrepreneurship/.

8. Ibid.

9. Amy Haimerl, "The Fastest-Growing Group of Entrepreneurs in America," http://fortune.com/2015/06/29/black-women-entrepreneurs/.

10. Ibid.

11. Ibid.

two-thirds of such enterprises have no woman of color on their boards. Women in general constitute 5 percent of Fortune 500 CEOs.[12] The number of African American CEOs in Fortune 500 companies is dismal to say the least. Currently there are only six African Americans executives serving in said positions.[13] Of the six, only one is a female, Ursula Burns. Burns has been Chair and CEO of Xerox Corporation since her appointment in 2010. The first African American woman in this position for any Fortune 500 company, Burns is also a mother.

In a blog featured in the *Wall Street Journal*, Ursula Burns offers this advice on motherhood and balancing the corporate conundrum:

> Don't take guilt trips. Mothers often feel pressure to be present for their children all the time, but such expectations are neither realistic nor necessary, Burns says. "Kids are pretty resilient," she says. "You don't have to be at every volleyball game. We can't guilt ourselves." Her own mother missed many of her extracurricular activities, she adds, "and I'm fine."[14]

Burns clearly hits on the challenges mothers in corporate America face. Many wrestle with choosing to play the "good ole boys" game or being a good mother. Burns's rise from an intern to the international face of Xerox has taught this lesson of not feeling guilty over missing a child's events. It a lesson for current-day mothers trying to juggle career and family.

Another African American mother "handling her business" is Rosalind Brewer. The next time you venture to Walmart or Sam's, think of this CEO. In 2012 Brewer took the reins as the first female president of Sam's Club, a division of the Walmart brand. When asked how she handles being a mom, wife, and businesswoman, Brewer offered these comments:

> I try to set priorities. I realize that I can't do it all. I find out what's important to me and to the business, and I have to prioritize. It takes almost every day to do that though. And learning how to say no. That I still fight with. Every now and then, my heart gets in the way and I can't help it.[15]

12. Ibid.

13. "Ursula M. Burns," Black Profiles, www.blackentrepreneurprofile.com/profile-full/article/ursula-m-burns/.

14. Leslie Kwoh, "Xerox CEO Ursula Burns Has Advice for Ambitious Women," *Wall Street Journal*, March 20, 2013, http://blogs.wsj.com/atwork/2013/03/20/xerox-ceo-ursula-burns-has-advice-for-ambitious-women/.

15. Heather Weekly, "Q and A: Sam's Club's Rosalind Brewer," *Capital Style*, January/February 2014, http://www.capital-style.com/content/stories/2014/01/business-savvy.html.

Brewer alludes to one aspect of motherhood that makes being out of the house difficult—the emotional tugs. Maternal instinct pulls women to want to be present at all times for their children. Yet for so many it is the professional pull that coerces women to find fulfillment by other means. I aver that some mothers need the compulsion of work both in and out of the home. The numbers are perhaps just as equal for mothers who deem full-time parenting work enough. Brewer is correct that the issue is to set priorities. I think this is sound for stay-at-home and got-to-go-to-work African American mothers.

Another African American mother with a Bathsheba effect is Faye Wattleton. For fourteen years Wattleton was the CEO of Planned Parenthood. She was the youngest, the first woman, and the first African American to hold the title in this nonprofit, from 1978 to 1992. It makes sense that a mother would be the leader of an organization identified as a reproductive health provider. More fascinating, and seemingly contradictory, is Wattleton's background as the daughter of a fundamentalist Church of God preacher. Like Bathsheba, she reconfigured her own story. Regarding motherhood, Wattleton asserts, "The future and strength of the race is for women to be able to have kids when they want them and to love and provide them with the tools they'll need to get through a hostile world. The image of the black woman bearing child upon child against her will is the real threat to the race."[16] Wattleton's work provided space for working women to decide about motherhood.

Wattleton's quote connects with Bathsheba's action in that the wife of a king has to ensure that Solomon has the "tools he needs to get through a hostile world." For Bathsheba, securing the kingdom and deracinating any and all threats to her son are her ways for providing for him. Wattleton's remarks are interesting, however, in that Bathsheba initially did not get to choose when to have children. Yet the biblical narrative purports that her second son with David, Solomon, was more of her volition.

I chose Burns, Brewer, and Wattleton because they represent significant milestones in corporate America and in motherhood. Burns is the only sitting African American woman of a Fortune 500 company. Brewer's connection with Sam's/Walmart is intriguing in light of the class dynamics connected to Walmart. Known for its low

---

16. Shawn D. Lewis, "Family Planning's Top Advocate," *Ebony Magazine* (September 1978): 86. https://books.google.com/books?id=TM0DAAAAMBAJ.

prices, the stores are primarily in impoverished, rural areas. They have recently gained notoriety for paying unfair wages and decided, after a heated battle, to increase employees' pay.[17] The fact that an African American woman guided Planned Parenthood intrigues me. An organization whose mission centers on reproductive health and giving women choices and the power to determine if they are ready for motherhood at one time had an African American woman at the helm.

CONCLUSION

The story of Bathsheba teaches many lessons through the lens of womanist maternal thought. First, mothers can rewrite their own stories. The text has Bathsheba silent for almost twenty years. When she reappears, she does so with political prowess and profound rhetoric. She was no longer the sexual victim but a key power player in a "game of thrones." Ursula Burns did not stay an intern; she rewrote her narrative to that of CEO. Second, Bathsheba teaches mothers that it is okay to advocate for our children. If we do not, we cannot be so sure that someone else will. Brewer counsels mothers to prioritize and select carefully. This entails learning when to say yes to certain meetings and when to announce no to particular business trips for the sake of the children. Third, this queen mother demonstrates that mothers today must have the foresight to see what lies ahead. Bathsheba knew what would happen if Adonijah remained on his self-proclaimed throne. She also discerned why it was dangerous for him to stay around during Solomon's reign. Wattleton points to a sociological and communal threat if African American women are not free to choose. African American mothers today would be wise to take note of the ways these mothers maneuvered in a man's world.

Questions for Discussion

1. What immediately comes to mind when you hear "Bathsheba"?
2. What does it mean: "Society likes a good story but *loves* the bad stuff."

17. Hiroko Tabuchi, "Walmart Raising Wage to at Least $9," *New York Times*, February 19, 2015, http://www.nytimes.com/2015/02/20/business/walmart-raising-wage-to-at-least-9-dollars.html?_r=0.

3. How would you describe women and their way with words?
4. Do you see yourself in Ursula Burns, Rosalind Brewer or Faye Wattleton? Why?
5. To be "fearless" is to be_____.

7

Mary: A Favor(less) Mother

Luke 1:26–38

Mama exhorted her children at every opportunity to "jump at de sun."
We might not land on the sun, but at least we would get off the ground.[1]
—Zora Neale Hurston

I was teaching a course on women and the New Testament when our discussion turned to the various Marys in the Bible. We counted at least seven women with the name. It was a common name in the first century and remains so two thousand years later. What was intriguing about our class conversation was that only two of the biblical women named Mary have been influential in changing the tenor of theology, biblical studies, and gender and sexuality education—Mary Magdalene and Mary the mother of Jesus.

The students and I were even more amazed to learn that much of the teaching in churches and seminaries has often pitted these two women against each other. Many preachers and educators have continuously recycled the image of Mary Magdalene as the consummate whore versus the iconic figure of Mary the mother of Jesus as the purest of the pure. These women share the same name, but they met different fates and very different representations. The more the church demonized Mary Magdalene, the more it elevated Mary the mother of Jesus. It was, indeed, a theological and social reversal.

There is much irony about the manner in which biblical scholars, pastors, teachers, theologians, and laypersons have tended to characterize Mary the mother of Jesus. First the Immaculate Conception does not pertain to her, but to her mother. Some traditions have held that

1. Zora Neal Hurston, *Dust Tracks on the Road* (New York: Harper Collins, 1942), 13.

73

the woman who gave birth to Mary was a virgin. Thus, this "purity the-ology" or virginal hermeneutics or interpretation is not based on Mary, but on ideas that her mother did not "know" a man. Additionally, scholars argue that a few Jewish polemics identify "Mary as a harlot who conceived Jesus out of wedlock." Thus, the emergence of Virgin Mary theology sought to counter this turbid imagery.[2] Such arguments need not diminish what many say is Mary's ecclesiological significance. There is no need to devalue Mary for the sake of elevating her mother in the same manner in which interpreters have muddied Mary Magda-lene to heighten the chastity of Mary the mother of Jesus.

The second point of irony is related to Luke's depiction of Mary. Interpretation must bring to the center the author's description of the encounter between Mary and Gabriel. Luke notes that Mary is from Nazareth. Nazareth is not a big city. Some say that perhaps it wasn't a city at all but a village. Its obscurity lies in the fact that it rarely surfaces in historical accounts. One never heard of people taking a vacation in Nazareth or owning time shares there. It was a small area where every-one knew everybody else.

What is further resounding is Mary's lack of regard for herself. She does not think so highly of her state of being. Mary is the portrait of innocence and obeisance. Those who have interpreted Mary seem to esteem her more than the Gospel account of her own identity and social status. The angel Gabriel proclaims to her that she is "favored." Yet Mary's response stands as "favorless."

Viewing Mary from a womanist maternal perspective allows the reader to examine issues of class, gender, and, yes, motherhood specific to her. Mary was not from a metropolis. She hailed from a lowly town. She even sings of her lowliness in the Magnificat (Luke 1:46–55). She was a woman living in a patriarchal society where men made the rules. Finally, Mary is a mother, a single mother who has an encounter with the divine.

TEXT SUMMARY

(Luke 1:26–38)

The Gospel of Luke introduces Mary as a virgin from Nazareth engaged to a man named Joseph. Verse 28 says, "Greetings, favored one! The

2. Brittany E. Wilson, "Mary and Her Interpreters," in *Women's Bible Commentary*, 3rd ed., ed. Carol A. New-som, Sharon H. Ringe, and Jacqueline E. Lapsley (Louisville, KY: Westminster John Knox Press, 2012), 513.

Lord is with you." The Message version says, "Good morning! You're beautiful with God's beauty—beautiful inside and out! God be with you." Maybe in our vernacular, we would say, "Hey, girlfriend, you know you got it goin' on. God's got your back."

However one chooses to engage in linguistic code-switching, the reader cannot overlook Mary's response. Mary does not say, "Thank you." Mary does not say, "I am beautiful. God made me this way." Mary does not say, "Yeah, I do kinda got it goin' on, don't I?" On the contrary, the text says that Mary is perplexed and confused. She is shaken and is shaking her head, "Are you talking to me? Is there somebody else in the room? Maybe there's another Mary. Me favored? Me beautiful? Me blessed?" Mary cannot handle the compliment; she does not want to receive the goodness given to her.

Luke's story continues. Gabriel presses Mary even more. This divine being tells her again in Luke 1:30, "You have found favor with God." In other words, "Just in case you did not comprehend the first time, get it the second time. You are beautiful. You are blessed. You are favored." Gabriel nixes leaving Mary in a state of confusion. God's messenger does not allow Mary to wallow in low self-esteem. God's conduit does not give up on Mary. God, as represented through Gabriel, will not sacrifice Mary's future for self-loathing and self-doubt.

Gabriel tells Mary she will conceive and give birth to the son of God:

> The child's name will be Jesus. The child's mission will be to save. In the lineage of his ancestors the child will reign. He will be great. In other words, the Son to come through the womb of you, a poor girl from Nazareth, living under Roman imperialism, will himself rule. The kingdoms of Rome will come and go, but the kingdom of your son will never end.
>
> (Luke 1:31–33, my translation)

Luke punctuates the class and sex dichotomy. Not only is Mary second class compared to her espoused, Joseph, who is from the lineage of King David, she is even second to her son. Jesus will have an everlasting kingdom. Mary is just from Nazareth, a small, secluded town.

Following much hesitation, Mary finally yields to the power of God. In verse 38 she tells Gabriel, tells God, "Here I am. I'm your servant. Do what you want to do. Let your word be made alive in me" (my translation). In this case she is the model first-century girl in that she yields to a power greater than herself. Luke employs the language of "slavery" again, disrobing and revealing class and gender inequity. Yes,

Mary is to conceive and give birth to one who will rule and reign. However, she must give birth in an earthly context "pregnant" with sociopolitical domination and exploitation.

Quite confident and excited that God has favored her, Mary goes to see Elizabeth and is to remain with her for three months. Before Mary can share her good news, Luke notes Elizabeth's joy and confirmation. Mary too expresses her excitement through the "Magnificat" or "Song of Exaltation" (Luke 1:46–55). She acknowledges her lowly state and expresses gratitude for this "high." The Mary who initially struggled with merely hearing a divine call now sings shouts of praises for what is and is to come.

MARY THEN

Although Mary is from a small, insignificant town, she is to marry a man from the line of David. Thus, the author from the outset establishes a class distinction between the mother and father of Jesus. Furthermore, the author gives insight into Mary's age: The Jewish betrothal practice took place before a girl reached twelve and a half. Therefore, as a virgin, Mary would have been a young girl of marriageable age without the benefit of sexual intercourse.

In the Greco-Roman world, women and men were not seen as different in kind; they were only different in degree. Yes, they were both human, but they were variegated forms of human. Men were the fully formed being, whereas women were a weaker, less developed type. Men were "higher" because they were formed perfectly in the womb. Women were "lower" because of their imperfect formation. This thinking centered primarily on genitalia: the male's outward, extending genitalia over against the inner curvature of the female sex organ was at the center of this differentiation. Thus, anatomy guided sociology. The reproductive organs that determined sex became the basis for gender role destination. As an underdeveloped man, the woman was the weaker human.[3]

Women in the Greco-Roman context held domestic roles and managed their households. Anything pertaining to family, the home, or children was their domain. The "weaker sex" controlled the inside while the stronger sex got to go out and play, literally and figuratively.

---

3. Bart Ehrman, "The Oppression of Women in Early Christianity," in *The New Testament: A Historical Introduction* (New York: Oxford University Press, 2004), 398.

Evaluation of Roman law concerning women shows that even wealthy women suffered restrictions on their mobility and freedom. They lacked real decision-making power, authority, and significant leadership roles. In this environment not even classism could trump sexism.[4]

To further fortify the "weaker" versus "stronger" ideology in social and familial patterns, Roman culture espoused the marriage of younger girls to older men. What we consider May–December romances formed the core of the Roman family. Such age distinctions codified patriarchy, patrimony, patrinomiality, and patrilineage. In other words, profound age differences between a husband and wife laid the foundation for a man doing whatever, whenever, however, and with whomever.[5]

In this first-century imperial context, patriarchy was the order of the day. Pax Romana, or the "Peace of Rome," brought peace only to certain Romans—that is, to male Romans. It did not allow for or provide an open forum for women to give a "piece" of their minds. This is the setting in which Luke writes of Mary, who is to be the mother of Jesus.

Although Mary was Jewish, Luke does not isolate her story from the Roman context. As he states in the prologue (1:1–3), Luke wants to establish an orderly or more historical account. Thus, he clearly wants to set his version of the story of Jesus within the strong arm of the Roman Empire. For Luke, Jews were relegated to Roman control and rule. Although Jews throughout the empire enjoyed extensive religious freedom, the political prowess of Roman domination left no stone unturned. Jews were free to worship and gather in synagogues at will. Women and girls were, perhaps, not so fortunate. Gender inequality and sexism had tentacles stretching from the macrocosm of Rome to the microcosm of Judaism.[6]

Thus, a girl in the Greco-Roman world was not so fortunate. Perhaps this gives the readers some idea of why Mary initially doubts and nearly refuses to hear the message Gabriel gives to her. She has trouble seeing herself as a fortunate or blessed being.

Some argue whether Mary is more astounded at the prominence of the birth or at the fact that, as a virgin, she will give birth at all. Is Mary more concerned about the birth process or about what or who results from the birth? Her primary concern is that she and Joseph are in the betrothal period and not having sexual relations. Gabriel quickly

4. Karen King, "Women in Ancient Christianity," *Frontline: From Jesus to Christ*, http://www.pbs.org/wgbh/pages/frontline/shows/religion/first/women.html.
5. Stephanie Buchanon Crowder, "Mary: The Mother of Jesus" *Just Women* 7, no. 2, (Spring 2015): 28.
6. Ibid.

replies that divine intervention is at play, as the Spirit will overshadow her. The overshadowing does not mean that the Holy Spirit impregnates Mary but that God is at work in this entire process. It is no different than God opening the wombs of Sarah or Hannah. God takes an active role in bringing God's Son into the world.

Within the Greco-Roman context, the idea of divine paternity—of divine beings mating with humans—was not uncommon. Mythologies were replete with accounts of gods conceiving with humans to produce superhuman beings with special powers.[7] Here again, one cannot dismiss the setting in which Luke produced his work. Members of his predominantly Gentile audience would be familiar with such stories. Luke's audience could relate to this aspect of divine-human relationships, because it was common in forms of Greco-Roman mythology.

On the contrary, whether one argues that the Spirit impregnates Mary or that God uses Joseph, the focus is that Mary finally concedes. Mary's Magnificat—or Song of Praise—reinforces the class dynamics in this passage. This Song of Poor (*anawim*, which is the Hebrew word for "poor ones") is akin to the song of Hannah in 1 Samuel 2:1–10 and the Song of Miriam in Exodus 15:21. The same God who enabled Hannah to conceive Samuel empowers a woman of Mary's low status to conceive one greater than Samuel.[8] Luke did not compose this song. It is a traditional hymn on behalf of the "poor of the Lord"— the children, widows, foreigners, and others economically and socially impoverished. The Lord lifts the poor and marginalized and brings down the rich and mighty.

Therefore, Mary no longer has to question whether she is fortunate or blessed. Her beginning is, indeed, not her ending. Whereas she starts the encounter with God doubting her own worthiness, she leaves with a song of praise, realizing that she is highly favored and quite fortunate, to say the least. There is favor in her lowliness (Luke 1:48).

Yet herein is another catch. Elizabeth is an aristocrat—high class and well-to-do as the wife of a priest. Mary is from the outback, the lower side, a little old place called Nowhere. However, God reverses their situation and lifts Mary up, with Elizabeth saying, essentially, "Mary what are you doing here? You are the mother of the Savior." Despite their differences in age—Mary is a young girl and Elizabeth is advanced

7. Bart Ehrman, "The Greco Roman World," in *A Brief Introduction to the New Testament* (New York: Oxford University Press, 2009), 18.

8. Stephanie Buckhanon Crowder, "Luke," in *True to Our Native Land: An African American New Testament Commentary*, ed. Brian K. Blount and Cain Hope Felder (Minneapolis: Fortress Press, 2007), 161.

in age—and despite their class distinctions—Mary is single and from Nazareth and Elizabeth is married to a priest in the hill country—these women are united in their gender roles. Luke positions them as two who are about to give birth within the Roman context. Their gestational states, as their political states, unite them.

Mary is fortunate in that as a pregnant teenager she is able to spend time with a sister-mother-girlfriend figure who consoles and counsels her for three months. She, who lacks much social and political privilege, has the gift of having someone walk with her through the first trimester of her pregnancy. She has the honor of having Elizabeth to support and nurture her during this critical juncture of her life. There is no baby-momma drama, just the love and care that only another woman can give. How fortunate for sure!

MARY NOW

There was a time when being pregnant and single was a shame. It was an act of disgrace to be worn with stigma and a modern-day "scarlet letter." In the twenty first century, when celebrities like Halle Berry, Nia Long and, yes, Lil' Kim give birth without a husband, it is as if times are a changing or have changed. Perhaps it is the class dynamic that makes this "okay." These women are not on welfare or dependent on food stamps or WIC to survive. Society tends to applaud and affirm African American single mothers in certain economic categories and with fame.

As rumors abound that there are supposedly seven times more men in the world than women, some women are choosing to have children before marriage, if they marry at all. They are foregoing the "traditional" path of dating, marriage, and childbirth. About 45 percent of single mothers have never married.[9] For some women, deciding to be a mother is important to their identity; the lack of a husband is not going to hinder their maternal drives.

The racial backdrop of single motherhood is telling. Seventy-two percent of African American children are born to single mothers. This eclipses the rates in other groups: "17 percent of Asians, 29 percent of whites, 53 percent of Hispanics, and 66 percent of Native Americans were born to unwed mothers in 2008, the most recent year for which

---

9. U.S. Census Bureau, Table C3, *Living Arrangements of Children Under 18 Years and Marital Status of Parents, by Age, Sex, Race, and Hispanic Origin and Selected Characteristics of the Child for All Children*, 2010, http://www. census.gov/population/www/socdemo/hh-fam/cps2010.html.

government figures are available. The rate for the overall U.S. population was 41 percent."[10] This is an element of the modern-day Mary. As previously mentioned, Mary is not married to Joseph. The conversation she has with Gabriel is without the presence of Joseph, the baby's daddy.

What is also alarming about the race perspective is the connection to poverty and economics. As earlier stated, Berry and Long are quite well off fiscally—as far as the media reports. However, they are not universally representative of African American single motherhood. Half of single African American mother families have an income less than $25,000. Only one third of single mothers receive any child support, and the average for this is about $300 a month.[11] This meager subsistence can lead to food insecurity and little to no health insurance. As mothers live in poverty, so do the children. Child poverty, in the short term, can lead to poor academic performance, and, in the long term, no graduation, joblessness, ill health.

Jesse Washington adds the following when discussing why African American women have children without marriage:

> The legacy of segregation means . . . many men are unprepared to compete for jobs. The drug epidemic sent numbers of black men to prison, and crushed the job opportunities . . . Women don't want to marry men who can't provide for their families, and welfare laws created a financial incentive for poor mothers to stay single. Another one of the conclusions is that women see motherhood as one of life's most fulfilling roles—a rare opportunity for love and joy, husband or no husband.[12]

For many this is the real issue: there is a higher percentage of children born out of wedlock in the black community because the number of unmarried women (mothers or not) has grown, while the number of married women has not.[13]

Today's financial challenges in single motherhood are similar to those in Mary's day. As Mary the mother of Jesus lived in a context in which she was "low" and poor, the majority of single-mother-headed households

10. Jesse Washington, "Blacks Struggle with 72 Percent Unwed Mothers Rate," http://www.nbcnews.com/id/39993685/ns/health-womens_health/t/blacks-struggle-percent-unwed-mothers-rate/#.VMmBAsZOpm1.

11. Timothy Casey, "Single Motherhood in the United States—A Snapshot (2012)," Legal Momentum, http://www.legalmomentum.org/sites/default/files/reports/single-mothers-snapshot_0.pdf.

12. Jesse Washington, "Blacks Struggle," http://www.nbcnews.com/id/39993685/ns/health-womens_health/t/blacks-struggle-percent-unwed-mothers-rate/#.VMmBAsZOpm1.

13. Ta-Nehisi Coates, "Understanding Out-of-Wedlock Births in Black America," The Atlantic, http://www.theatlantic.com/sexes/archive/2013/06/understanding-out-of-wedlock-births-in-black-america/277084/.

today are in dire straits. Bette Dickerson asserts that there is confusion over the definition of single households. There may be individuals sharing a common dwelling, which she labels a "household." This condition is contrary to family members not living with the single parent who also play a significant role in childrearing. Thus, there is a communal approach to the single "household" functioning.[14]

Stats surrounding the percentage of children born to African American single mothers include teenaged mothers. They too are the "Mary" of this time. The birth rate for teenagers fifteen to nineteen has dropped 6 percent; yet this birth rate for this age group is not zero. For African Americans (fifteen to nineteen years old), the birth rate is forty-four births per one thousand, which is twice that of whites but less than Hispanic girls.[15] They are teen mothers who often live with their mothers, aunts, grandmothers, or guardians. Hence, Dickerson's push to redefine "household" is instructive. Like Mary, adolescent mothers need an "Elizabeth" to help them navigate this new state of their lives.

CONCLUSION

Sometimes we women get Maryitis—we cannot take a compliment. We do not allow ourselves to receive a good word. The wounds of life can be so profound and we can become so jaded that it is hard for us to accept any niceties. Like Mary, we doubt our worth and repel anyone who would tell us otherwise. Especially as African American mothers we beat ourselves up for not being able to provide all of the things we think our children need. The focus of some single mothers on keeping a roof overhead, providing clothes, and preparing a meal keeps them from receiving some good for themselves. Maryitis is to blame.

The text describes Gabriel as staying with Mary until she reverses her thinking about herself. It is not until Mary is convinced, not until Mary holds her head up, not until Mary gets on board that Gabriel departs. God will not leave us "stuck on stupid" and forces us to move to the next level, sometimes scratching and fighting. God sticks with us until we dare to reverse our self-perception. God plans so much more for us than we could ever have the courage to envision for ourselves.

---

14. Bette Dickerson, *African American Single Mothers: Understanding Their Lives and Families,* (Thousand Oaks, CA: SAGE, 1995), xiv.

15. Centers for Disease Control and Prevention, "Births: Final Data for 2012," http://www.cdc.gov/nchs/data/nvsr/nvsr62/nvsr62_09.pdf#table06.

God's choosing Mary has more to do with God's possibility and less to do with her virginity. Yes, she is fortunate, and she also has divine favor. "For nothing will be impossible with God" (Luke 1:37).

Not only does Mary have God's grace and indwelling, she has another soon-to-be mother to walk with her. Elizabeth can physically empathize with Mary's state as a woman and as an expectant mother. Women need other women to walk in our shoes, whether those shoes are Nine West, Target, Walmart, Cole Hahn, Gucci, or Payless. We need to be with each other. African American teens need mentors to help them journey through the craziness that is teenaged life. They especially require nurturing if they get pregnant. Their bodies may engage in grown woman acts, but their adolescent minds lag behind the physical prowess.

Elizabeth is not upset. She is not jealous or envious. Elizabeth does not say to Mary, "You've changed. You're not the same. Just because you are carrying the Savior of the world, who do you think you are?" Elizabeth does not play the class card and bark, "You're just Mary from the ghetto. I remember your trailer-park days." No, Elizabeth lauds, "Mary, God's going to produce something great in you. God's even producing in me." The same Redeemer, who Mary is carrying, will deliver Elizabeth just as he will redeem the entire world.

All women need an Elizabeth. Viewing the Mary-Elizabeth kinship through a womanist maternal lens shows how their class distinctions did not preclude them from being there for each other. Gender identification as mothers-to-be solidified their connection and dismantled any classism. African American mothers in the suburbs and African American mothers living in the ghetto must not let economics keep them from holding on to each other. Those with power and prestige still need to advocate for others on the margins. One cannot forget the triple consciousness of family, work, and community exemplified by Ida B. Wells and Mary Church Terrell. As African American women and African American mothers, they did not relinquish their public duty. Wells "nursed her two sons, taking them on trains on the way to her lectures."[16] A spirit of Ubuntu, I am because we are, compels this camaraderie. Truth is that society still places all African American women at the bottom of the social and class ladder.

We must have an Elizabeth who will support and affirm us. We need an Elizabeth to console and to counsel us. We must find someone

---

16. Lonnae O'Neal Parker, *I'm Every Woman: Remixed Stories of Marriage, Motherhood and Work* (New York: HarperCollins, 2005), 33.

who will be in our corner and urge us on. Even today, it is imperative to covenant with another woman whom we can go to, learn from, and grow with in our most fragile states. We cannot afford the gossip, backbiting, and "hateration" that can get in the way of our supporting each other. Although such activity is not limited to women, to mothers, it can be a hindrance to our work together. We all need to secure an Elizabeth for the sake of our well-being. And, dare I say, each of us needs to be an Elizabeth to another teen somewhere in this world.

In order to reverse our fortune, we must begin by reversing how we think of ourselves. We must reverse how we think of each other. There is a Mary in you. There is an Elizabeth in you. Walk in this favor.

Questions for Discussion

1. Mary's doubtful response is, "How can this be, since I am a virgin?" (Luke 1:34). Describe a time when you believed God was calling you to do something you weren't sure you could do.
2. Who has been an Elizabeth for you? For whom have you been an Elizabeth?
3. Mary, just a teenager, was an unwed mother. How does this relate to how society currently views pregnant teens or unwed pregnant women in general?
4. Sometimes we women get Maryitis—we cannot take a compliment. What makes us suspicious when people say good things about us?
5. What does it mean to be "favorless"?

8

The Canaanite Woman:
A Relentless Mother

Matthew 15:21–28

We pray/accept responsibility for children [and mothers] who live and
move, . . . but have no being.
                    —"A Prayer for Our Children" (Ina Hughes adapted by
                                                Marian Wright Edelman)[1]

To work or not to work? That is the question? Even before the economic crash of 2008, family members were already assessing whether
one income was enough. It did not take bailouts of corporate entities
or the housing market debacle for some to examine their fiscal security.
It is almost a middle-class given that in a two-parent household both
contribute to the money coffers. Perhaps the days of mommy staying
at home are over or becoming more obsolete. Money is tight, and all
able bodies are on deck.

    If an individual household is in the 1 percent of the population
controlling all of the nation's wealth, then there are maternal options
when it comes to working. Class has a way of impacting which mothers go to work and which chose to stay at home. If a typical middle-
class household had to weather a period of joblessness without any
income, they would exhaust their available savings within twenty-one
days. If that same family also cashed in all their retirement invest-
ments, they would burn through those assets within four months.[2]
There are exceptions, and families have unique dynamics. Bette
Dickerson is correct: "There is no one form of the African American family but rather a range of structures that meet people's needs

---

1. Marian Wright Edelman, "A Prayer for Our Children," in *Guide My Feet* (Boston: Beacon Press, 2013), 108.
2. Associated Press via *Chicago Tribune* wire reports, "Almost Half of U.S. Households Exhaust Their Salaries," http://www.chicagotribune.com/business/breaking/chi-households-exhaust-salaries-20150129-story.html.

at various points in their lives or that may be forced on them by circumstances."[3]

Working outside of the home or working in the house is still work. It requires time, effort, diligence, and much patience. Organizations like Mocha Moms show that African American mothers are forgoing work away from home.[4] Whereas connecting such activity to white middle-class mothers is historical, African American mothers are now a part of this group. Although there is a class factor and a race element, much of the polemic between mothers at home and mothers not home is centered around childcare and the level of trust attached to it. Both sets of mothers work to ensure that their children have proper supervision and attention.

Perhaps the crux of the matter is redefining the definition of work to include both mothers whose nine-to-five is at their residence and those who punch a clock at work. Patricia Collins states: "Working is as parallel with motherhood. It is an important and valued dimension of motherhood. Work contributes to children's values and instills in them a force to do better. It helps to transcend boundaries."[5] In this study of womanist maternal thought I define work as the consistent, conscientious act of pursuing those in power and challenging authority for survival, healing, health, wholeness, and future security. This is the primary, life-giving, life-affirming work all mothers must do—advocacy rooted in African American communal motherhood and mothers who stay at home to work it out.

The story of the Canaanite mother in the Gospel of Matthew helps in presenting this new understanding of a working mother. Although this narrative also occurs in Mark 7:24–30 (known as the Syrophoenician mother), I chose Matthew's version because of the negative "Canaanite" descriptive the author applies to the mother and the way in which the disciples reject her, urging Jesus to send her away. I also found intriguing the concept of faith as evident in Matthew and lacking in Mark's version. For Matthew, the Canaanite woman's faith is expressed through her mediating on behalf of another—in this case, her daughter. Thus, work is rooted in the fruit of one's faith.

3. Bette Dickerson, *African American Single Mothers: Understanding Their Lives and Families*, (Thousand Oaks, CA: SAGE, 1995), x.

4. See www.mochamoms.org.

5.Patricia Hill Collins, *Black Feminist Thought*, 2nd ed. (New York: Routledge, 2000), 184.

TEXT SUMMARY

(Matthew 15:21–28)

Matthew records that Jesus and the disciples are traveling in Tyre and Sidon. They are in the area of Phoenicia, many miles north of Judah. On their way, they meet a woman who comes shouting and screaming after Jesus. She does not address the disciples but pleads to Jesus for mercy. Her daughter has a demon.

Jesus does not offer any verbal, physical, or emotional comfort. He is silent. The disciples, whom the woman was not addressing, tell Jesus to send the woman away. They exclaim, "she keeps shouting after us" (v. 23). At this point Jesus answers the woman, "I am not here for you, but for the house of Israel. You are an outsider" (v. 24, my translation).

The mother, changing her posture, kneels before Jesus and engages in a tête-à-tête with him. Jesus does not ameliorate the situation; instead it gets metaphorically worse. He tells the woman that she is a dog, and dogs should not receive the children's food. In other words, what he has come to offer the children of Israel does not belong to the Canaanite dogs in Phoenicia. The mother is relentless. She does not give up and grovels for even the bread crumbs from the children. Basically, she tells Jesus to do for her child how little you want; just do *something*. Jesus acquiesces. He tells the woman that her faith is profound. Because of this mother's relentless work, her daughter is healed instantly.

CANAANITE MOTHER THEN

Matthew establishes Jesus, a Jew, as entering the northern districts of Tyre and Sidon, which are under Roman rule. He encounters the Canaanite woman in this predominately Gentile territory. For Matthew's readers, this Canaanite is a reminder of the people God had to drive out in order for Abraham's descendants to receive the promise. She is a reminder of an idolatrous people who did not honor the God of Abraham, Isaac, and Jacob. The author's mention of "Canaanite" also recalls the Matthean genealogy of Jesus, which lists other Canaanite women: Tamar (Matt. 1:3) and Rahab (Matt. 1:5). Both Tamar and Rahab are outsiders associated with prostitution and sexual deviance. All three women achieve their goals through skillful speech and deed while acknowledging Israel's precedence in salvation history.

The Canaanite mother is the first woman to speak to a male in the

Gospel of Matthew. Yes, Herodias tells her daughter to request the head of John the Baptist (Matt. 14:8); however, the Canaanite mother is the first woman to speak to Jesus in this Gospel. Yes, the bleeding woman encounters Jesus, but she talks to herself and never responds to him (Matt. 9:18–26). Matthew mentions mothers (1:18–25), a mother-in-law (8:14–15), and motherhood (10:35–37; 12:46–50). However, until this literary pause, no woman speaks to Jesus other than this ethnic outsider.

Although Jesus is in an area where he is the racial minority, Matthew employs language that depicts him otherwise. Jesus has power; the Canaanite woman wants to access it. Her physical actions demonstrate subordination because she beseeches Jesus on her knees. Using a rhetoric of marginalization, her language further perpetuates powerlessness and class subjugation, even in her own hometown. She refers to Jesus as "Lord" three times (15:22, 25, 27). He is the "Son of David," an acknowledgment of the magnificence of Hebrew history (15:22). Jesus initially ignores the woman's presence and does not answer her at all (15:23). His disciples try to convince him to send her away because she is making too much noise (15:24).

Jesus calls the woman a "dog" (15:26), a derogatory term the Canaanite woman then uses to refer to herself (15:27). Perhaps Matthew repeats the reference as a play on the Greek words for dog (*kynaria*) and Canaanite (*Chananaia*). This "dog" only wishes for crumbs from the master's table (15:27). Finally, the Canaanite woman does not have a name. She is merely a woman who comes out and starts shouting at Jesus—or a loose street dog who would not stop barking. Musa W. Dube substantiates this point: "to characterize a foreign woman as a 'Canaanite' is to mark her as one who must be invaded, conquered, annihilated. . . . She must survive only as a colonized mind, a subjugated and domesticated subject."[6] As a colonized woman the Canaanite lives in an area under Roman rule. Her people are not free to do as they wish. They live in a territory taken over by Rome via war. Thus, they are subjects and subjugated to Roman authority. Colonization impacts physical activity, and according to Dube's previous quote, it can also influence mental liberty. If one is constantly forced to move and be at the whims of others, such limitations are bound to break mental wherewithal.

As womanist maternal thought examines motherhood through class dynamics, one can see how this mother is caught in the middle of a game of social status for the sake of her daughter. She is merely an

---

6. Musa W. Dube, *Postcolonial Feminist Interpretation of the Bible* (St. Louis: Chalice Press, 2000), 147.

animal. Additionally it is a male who questions this woman's class. Thus, the gender element of womanist maternal thought is also present. Jesus is the perpetrator of these classist and sexist ideologies.

The Canaanite woman shouts at Jesus and pleads for mercy. She does not ask for anything nonessential. Her request involves life and death. She does not desire to kill a man, like Herodias, the mother in Matthew 14:1–12; nor does she desire a place in the kingdom of God, like the mother of the sons of Zebedee in Matthew 20:20–28. Her daughter is demon-possessed and needs deliverance. Her baby is not herself, and momma has done all she knows how to do. So the Canaanite woman goes to work.

The Canaanite woman works. She actively pursues Jesus because she believes that, as the "Lord" and "Son of David," he has power. She works in that she does not stop shouting or pleading with Jesus to use his power to enhance her situation, even when the disciples urge him to send her away. This mother works relentlessly so that her demon-possessed daughter may survive and experience wholeness. This mother works her faith and secures not only a present healing but a future promise initially reserved for the house of Israel. Her persistence paid off not only for her, but for generations to come.

The Canaanite mother sacrifices her body insofar as she dares to speak so boldly to a man in public in a patriarchal society. After all, Matthew does not say she is under anyone's authority; thus, someone in authority could reprimand her for "out of place" actions. The author does not mention a husband; so perhaps the Canaanite is a single mom. Nonetheless, she puts her mental acumen and emotions on the table as she engages in a verbal contest with Jesus and yields to his language of marginalization for the sake of her daughter. Her work is a sacrifice of her physical, emotional, and mental self. Yet, in the end, she also reaps spiritual benefits. The Canaanite woman's faith spurs action, and her action brings healing to her child.

CANAANITE MOTHERS NOW

A few years ago, I had the privilege of attending the Samuel DeWitt Proctor conference at Haley Farm in Clinton, Tennessee. Samuel DeWitt Proctor was President of Virginia Union University and had taught at several colleges, universities, and seminaries. The Children's Defense Fund created a conference in his honor. It was hot and muggy under the tent, even with the fans blowing. The speakers were thought-provoking. The music was inspiring. The meals were tasty. And yes, the heat was sweltering. I was there because I believe in the mission and work of the Children's Defense Fund.

Marian Wright Edelman, founder of the Children's Defense Fund, started this grassroots organization over forty years ago.[7] The purpose is to bring attention to the plight of children. The CDF and Edelman are a constant reminder that the United States must change its policies and raise its standards when it comes to children's well-being.

Edelman not only has a history in the civil rights movement, but as a lawyer, she provided counsel to Martin Luther King Jr. and assisted with what would have been the Poor People's Campaign. She spends days on Capitol Hill making sure that Congress does not forget about the children. Edelman is also a mother, and she knows what it means to advocate for not only her children but all children.

Work is the consistent, conscientious act of pursuing those in power and challenging authority for survival, healing, health, wholeness, and future security. It is relentless advocacy. To work, with or without financial remuneration, is not only to seek my welfare but to seek the well-being of persons in my family, my community, and the world. Work is active, not passive. It is what I/we do, not what is done to me/us. Such work requires the engagement and cooperation of mind, body, and spirit. This definition of work maintains that stay-at-home mothers engage in work, challenges, and advocacy. Mediation and intervention take different shapes and forms.

Work is thus more than a reluctant, "I've got to go to work": it is an intense, focused, determined "I've got work to do!", because life and soul are at stake. The work mothers do on behalf of their children has a spiritual element.[8] This wholistic work benefits mothers who are able to provide for their children and benefits the children as recipients of their mother's efforts. The Canaanite woman's faith spurs action, and her action also brings healing to her child.

Whether a black mother who works faces any extra challenges is still debatable. Some may think that working mothers stunt a child's mental, emotional, physical, social, or spiritual growth. In all fairness, other related variables lead to further discussion.

However, the variations of maternal machinations can cause

7. See http://www.childrensdefense.org/.
8. Teresa L. Fry Brown, *God Don't Like Ugly: African American Women Handing on Spiritual Values* (Nashville: Abingdon Press, 2000), 59.

working and nonworking mothers to view the other as outsiders. Outsider language not only seeks to subjugate a person's rights; it also moves to challenge an individual's authority. Outsider language is a rhetoric of subversion that says to a professional, "Yes, you are the doctor with a medical degree from Harvard, Vanderbilt, or Yale, but I want a second and third opinion. Are you sure about this diagnosis?" Outsider language is the government's welfare system penalizing our inner-city moms if the baby's daddy lives with them while persons with privilege get welfare in the form of tax breaks, bailouts, and subsidies. This bureaucratic behavior is unacceptable.

Outsider maternal language says, "What does an African American mother mean when she says she is a stay-at-home mother, home schooling her children? Doesn't she work?" Outsider language says to African American mothers who work, "Why don't you stay at home? Daycares are not the place for children. Don't you miss out on their development when you work? Doesn't your husband make enough? Do you have a husband?" Such language precludes the one on the outside, the one on the margins, from ever advancing or winning. Nothing this person does or is ever will be the right thing to do or be. Even on our own grounds, in our native land, minding our own business, we African American women, like this Canaanite woman, can speak to reversals of power. Not wanting to be too presumptuous, it is possible that women in other racial and ethnic marginalized categories can connect with this as well.

This portrait of African American motherhood through the study of the Canaanite mother is broad enough to even cover various mothers who specialize in tough love, perhaps lending themselves to the "mean mommy" nomenclature. Yet readers are perhaps more comfortable with the nurturing, caring, doting type of mommy. Regardless, one can see that the continuum of mothering is wide indeed.

CONCLUSION

Where do we go from here? I think this contemporary analysis of the work of the Canaanite mother as a prototype of black working mothers and perhaps mothers in general leads to many places. First, professionally we must talk more about family as integral to our career identity. Many of us bring our families to professional meetings; however, there is limited discussion on the intersection of family and career. We cannot overlook the "off the record" questions at job interviews about family or plans for children. Issues of marriage, maternal obligations, and family leave are the elephants in the boardroom.

Second, I maintain that a womanist maternal interpretation takes up the mantle of race not addressed in feminism; it must do more to highlight internal class issues between African American mothers who work downtown and African American mothers who cook in and clean the high rise offices. Work or "advocacy" also means giving voice to African American mothers on welfare, mothers who are the working poor, and mothers who work for other African American mothers.

Finally, we must address the children. If one surmises that the Canaanite mother leaves her child home alone, then the daughter is a latchkey child. She is a child who in our modern time has a key to the house and enters an empty home to fend for herself until mother arrives. Work must advocate for after-school networks, faith-based initiatives, and community programs to fill in the gap. Work means issuing clarion calls to strengthen existing programs where surrogate mothers and neighborhood grandmothers step in until momma gets off work.[9]

It will work, if we work it!

Questions for Discussion

1. Who are the present-day disciples who try to "send people away" and prevent their wholeness and healing?
2. What is your response to the way in which Jesus initially replies to the Canaanite mother?
3. African American mothers work to tear down the walls of racism, classism, and sexism for the sake of their children. How does the work you do (paid or unpaid) confront these issues?
4. What does it mean to be "relentless" in one's work or efforts?
5. What do you think causes the tension between mothers who stay at home and mothers who work outside the home?

9. Stephanie Buckhanon Crowder, "The Canaanite Woman," *Just Women.* 7, no. 2 (Spring 2015): 37.

9

Zebedee's Wife: A Shameless Mother

Matthew 20:20–28

I am #womanistmomma. I am a #sportsmomma.
                                   —Stephanie Buckhanon Crowder

As far as his mother was concerned, Bobby was the best player on the soccer team. He came to every practice on time. With cleats laced, gloves in hand, Gatorade in tow, he was always willing to go the extra mile. Bobby had a good attitude. He constantly cheered for his teammates even when they did not do so well. They could count on Bobby to say, "It's alright. It's okay." Bobby cheered for his peers game after game—from the bench.

Bobby would get to play once in a while, but this was high school. Everybody was just as good if not better. Nonetheless, this reality did not sit so well with Bobby's mother, Mrs. Toll. She could no longer take having her "best athlete in the world" ride the wood. Her son had professional soccer ability. The family needed Bobby to make it. At least, this is what pervaded Momma Toll's mental machinations. She had had enough. She was desperate. Her baby needed security. Her boy needed to be on that soccer field. So she asked. After a game, she approached Coach Moore and inquired, "Can Bobby get more playing time?"

This is fictional. Yet there is much truth here that speaks to what mothers will do on behalf of their children. Mothers will ask whomever, for whatever, whenever if it will benefit a son or daughter. Sometimes what mothers request will covertly serve their well-being.

The mother of James and John, the wife of Zebedee, makes a request of Jesus. Although her request is not as simple as more time running up and down a field, it is significant to her nonetheless. No, James and John's mother does not have at stake a Nike endorsement, but her longing is rooted in some degree of security. She does not seek prime time in the playoffs, but her desire is for prime positions in God's kingdom. Whereas Mrs. Toll and Mrs. Zebedee are millennia apart, their maternal efforts to obtain the best for their children cross the chasm of time. They want what any mother pines for: assurance that their children will have what momma thinks they need.

Sometimes what mothers think their children need may not be what they really need. Perhaps this Bible story walks on egg shells in its description of Mrs. Zebedee. Yet moms have to be honest that they can be scary beings when it comes to their babies. As "Grannies" and "Nanas," they can be formidable opponents on the field, in the house, in the church, in the store, and on the Internet. Even the sweetest "Aunt Bess" can become a beast if a person dares to mess with her niece or nephew. One reason is that parents, grandparents, and adults tend to live vicariously through their children and younger family members. There, I said it. Confession is good for the soul. Now rise and be healed!

This lesson of the mother of James and John helps readers to see the games mothers play. "Games" refer to the lengths people go for the sake of others, especially family members. It is the extent of shameless advocacy or mediation for the benefit of those we love. "Games" can have a pejorative connotation if such acts are harmful or parasitic. However, this study does not purport that the "games" are bad. After all, the mother of James and John just wanted security for her children. She wanted assurance that in a society where fishing was not a lucrative business, her sons would be okay. Thus if Jesus were talking about kingdom business, surely that must have been better than the fishing business. So "game on" according to Mrs. Zebedee! "He asked my sons to follow him (Matt. 4:21), and they did. Now let's see what they get in return." Game recognizes game. Let the playing begin.

TEXT SUMMARY

(Matthew 20:20–28)

Jesus is traveling with the disciples throughout Judah. He is headed toward Jerusalem and approaching death via crucifixion. The Gospel of Matthew maintains Jesus has just foretold his death for the third time (20:17–19). Immediately at this moment, the mother of James and John, the sons of Zebedee, along with her sons, approaches Jesus. Begging on her knees, she asks him a favor. Jesus asks the mother what she wants.

This nameless mother, whom I call Mrs. Zebedee, states that she wants her sons to have prime positions in Jesus' kingdom. She would like for one to sit at his right hand and the other to sit at his left hand on the throne. Jesus does not answer her. Instead, he asks the sons if they are able to handle what their mother thinks they should have. "Can you really drink the cup, drink from the cup, I am about to drink?" (my translation) is the question the soon-to-be-dead Jesus poses to these disciples. Without hesitation, both sons respond, "Absolutely!"

Jesus affirms that yes the disciples will drink his cup (i.e., die) but concedes that he cannot grant the kingdom request. He tells the mother and sons that what they want is not his to give. The kingdom and the choice of seat selection belong to God.

This is not the end of the story. The other ten disciples are pretty furious with James and John. Jesus steps in to calm tempers. He tells the disciples the primary lesson of the entire exchange: greatness comes not from being the head or on top; it lies in service to humankind. The power is not in the position but in the attitude associated with servanthood.

To borrow the word of the late ESPN analyst Stuart Scott: Boo-Yah!

MRS. ZEBEDEE THEN

What becomes apparent in examining the literary development of mothers in the Gospel of Matthew is that they become more bold, more audacious, and more aggressive. In each stage the Gospel presents mothers moving from quiet acquiescence to effrontery-filled action and demand. From negotiating healing to plotting a decapitation to requesting the best seats in the kingdom of heaven, Matthew's mothers show a progression of the power and prowess embedded in the maternal figure. If one follows this characterization of the mothers, the requests of the mother of James should not be surprising

Instead of being offended by Mrs. Zebedee's request, one understands the context for her requests. It appears that Jesus had set them up. Matthew provides much detail about Jesus' relationship with James and John. Matthew 4 notes much narrative about Jesus calling them out of fishing with bait to fishing for humanity. Matthew 10 lists them as numbers 3 and 4 among the disciples. They are with Peter and Jesus on the Mount of Transfiguration in Matthew 17. Their eyes behold Elijah. They gaze toward Moses. Even after the fact (chapter 26), James and John are with Jesus in the Garden of Gethsemane. They are asleep, but they are there.

Not every disciple was privy to such moments in the ministry of Jesus. Everybody did not get an invitation to the transfiguration. So do we blame James, John, and Momma for trying to take the relationship one step further? Yes, it is possible that she mistook Jesus' cues. You have heard it said that we do not see things as they are; we see them as we are. As far as she was concerned, Mrs. Zebedee's sons needed to see the kingdom! This exercise dares not suggest that Jesus is toying with the lives of James, John, or their mother. According to Matthew, Jesus is serious about the kingdom of heaven belonging to all—including the poor, tax collectors, and fishermen. Matthew's Jesus is an equal opportunity savior, deliverer, and provider.

People are human. Matthew notes this humanity and this reality. The author records the birth of Jesus through a human. The text is replete with encounters with humans. Jesus dies at human hands. He appears to humans at the resurrection and commissions them in the end. Thus, incorporated in this literature are stories of the mother of James and John and other mothers acting and behaving as only humans, made in God's image, can act.

Surprisingly, Mrs. Zebedee, who makes a bold plea of Jesus, is nameless in this story. Matthew does not name all of the mothers, and conditions under which the mothers warrant naming is unclear. Of course Mary the mother of Jesus has a name. Perhaps Herodias's affiliation and association with the politically laden Herodian family as outlined in Matthew 2 warrants her naming. Yet the same level of audacious request is present in both Herodias and Mrs. Zebedee. However, Matthew names one and not the other. The author cues the reader into ways in which the author is influenced by the sociopolitical imperialistic force that is the Roman government. Matthew is not shy about pointing directly to the powers that be, and Herodias has access to such power.

Notwithstanding, the mother of James and John is not bashful nor does she mince words. She is clearly calculating in her request. Intriguingly enough, there are degrees of irony with what she says, how she says it, and when she says it. First, her timing seems a little, well, inopportune. Matthew notes that Jesus has just foretold his pending, brutal death for the third time (20:17–19). Jesus makes it clear that he will die; he will die a heinous death via crucifixion. Jesus tells his followers he will suffer like a common criminal, guilty of treason against the Roman Empire.

Immediately following this revelation is the request of Mrs. Zebedee. Jesus has just forecast his death, and the mother of James of John asks for kingdom territory. Matthew records an ensuing beating and betrayal while this mother wants security for her boys. Surely no mother would want her children to have any parts of someone's death, especially death by crucifixion.

Matthew is intentional in this literary positioning. Not only does Jesus preview his death, the writer pens his resurrection as well. Although Jesus in Matthew shares his impending death on three occasions, he also uplifts his life after death. This is what attracts the mother of James and John. Yes, Jesus will die. However, Jesus will also live again. "If he is to live again, then he truly is some type of divine king, and I want my sons to have a share in this kingdom." The nature of her request and her presence at the crucifixion (27:55–56) is Matthew's way of demonstrating that the mother of James and John was also a follower of Jesus. Mrs. Zebedee was a constant companion with Jesus and the disciples.[1] She traveled with them. Thus there was a degree of familiarity with her presence.

Furthermore, Jesus responds to this mother with an open-ended question. He asks her what she wants. I posit that this also implies a degree of familiarity between the two. It is as if this mom is so close to Jesus and believes in him so much that she wants her sons to have not just eternal life but a piece of the kingdom action on earth. This connection with the request to kingdom and death is very similar to the move Bathsheba makes when David is on his deathbed. This mother asks for the kingdom for her son. As Matthew's genealogy includes Bathsheba and David, the parallels are likely not coincidental.[2]

In addition to her strange timing, Mrs. Zebedee's physical posture is peculiar and ironic. What she asks and the style of the question are contradictory. In the Greek, the word *proskyneo* describes her action. In essence, she begs, kneeling before Jesus. The connotation for this word also implies desperation or urgency. It is the same word Matthew

---

1. Amy-Jill Levine, "The Gospel of Matthew," in *Women's Bible Commentary*, 2nd ed. (Louisville, KY: Westminster John Knox Press, 2012), 465.

2. "The Gospel according to Matthew," Catholic Study Bible (NAB), Oxford Biblical Studies Online, http://www.oxfordbiblicalstudies.com/article/sidebyside/bibref/NAB/commref/NAB/Mt/20#verse20.

uses to describe the visit of the Magi (2:2, 8), the ruler pleading for his daughter's life (9:18), the disciples' cries during the stilling of the storm (14:33), and the Canaanite mother's request (15:25). Except for the adoration of the Magi, all of these instances wreak of a pressing matter.

I purport that imperativeness for the mother of James and John is connected to their state as fishermen. When Jesus summoned the two (4:21–22), they were with their father mending their nets. Matthew writes that the sons leave Zebedee and immediately follow Jesus. First-century fishermen were despised and lowly, belonging to a "middle poor." "Fishermen . . . could not determine how much they earned, as there was a political and economic system that regulated taxation. Any subsequent remaining profit went to the elite and those who controlled the fishing process from the top. Thus the system was not one that allowed for entrepreneurship or capitalism as in our modern-day thinking. It was a matter of fishing to eat and survive."

"In addition, persons in the fishing industry depended on people in various professions to help supply nets, boats, and other needed materials. Processors, distributors, buyers, and sellers partnered with those whose primary responsibility it was to catch fish. Thus fishing was not an individual commercial endeavor. It was one grounded in relationships akin to present-day unions."

"Jesus speaks to the [fishermen] on their own terms. . . . Jesus does not discount their profession or place in society. On the contrary, he calls them and commands them to rethink their position, in order that they might help others to do the same. Jesus does not ask any of the men in the text to follow him. Instead, he issues an imperative, a command. The irony is that perhaps many Roman officials had commanded Peter, Andrew, James, and John to go and/or to do something. They were residing in Capernaum of Galilee, an area under the political auspices of King Herod's son, Herod Antipas. Soldiers and military personnel populated the area in order to ensure civil obedience and to dissuade any who might consider uprising. Thus the people residing in the territory were accustomed to commands delivered with physical and even verbal insults."[3]

"Hence although her timing is questionable and her posture is poor and degrading, the mother of James and John makes a kingdom plea for sake of trying to give her sons position in a new world order. She desires that they move up and out of their places at the bottom of the

3. Stephanie Buckhanon Crowder, *Feasting on the Gospels: Matthew* (Louisville, KY: Westminster John Knox Press, 2013), 1:63–67.

social ladder into the second and third positions of power in the kingdom of God. Her present condition as a fisherman's wife motivates her to do something for the sake of her boys. She wants a better life for her sons and takes any means necessary for them to have more and be more. She and her family have come to know the social, economic, and political limitations of the Rome and its kings. She now risks signing on with Jesus and his kingdom. Yet, one wonders if the mother really understood 'kingdom' as Jesus articulated 'kingdom.'"

"Mrs. Zebedee seems to think of kingdom in terms of the Roman Empire. Her frame of reference is the power, prestige, authority of emperors, soldiers, war, conscription, and political machinations. Her situation is colored by social marginalization and economic depravity. For this mother, kingdom is a force to be overthrown and overtaken. The Peace of Rome, or Pax Romana, has not been peaceful. Thus, another kingdom must come to rid the world of it."[4]

On the contrary this is not how Matthew's Jesus presents "kingdom." Matthew employs "God's kingdom" only five times. However, the writer makes the point of imperial expectation and restoration clear in that "kingdom of heaven" appears in over thirty verses in Matthew. Consequently for Matthew's primarily Jewish audience, the idea of God ruling here and now is more profound. From Matthew 3:2 to 26:29, "kingdom" language speaks not just of an ethereal ideology, but it is rooted in the authoritarian dis-ease in the author's context.

Jesus produces a game of "show and tell" to make his point regarding the kingdom of heaven as a kingdom of reversal. The image of a little child sitting among disciples serves to reinforce the idea of God's rule over against Roman rule (18:2). In a society where children held no political power, were the most vulnerable, and at the bottom of the social ladder, Jesus presents a new world rooted in childlike action and faith (19:14–15). Furthermore, not only is humility in heart at the core of this new reign, but there must be a willingness to share one's good. Such could be problematic for the rich in Matthew's world who were accustomed to hoarding for themselves (19:23).

Thus where the mother of James and John thinks of subjugating the Roman government, Jesus avows kingdom in terms of reversing the social order. Interestingly enough both ideas of "kingdom" have at the core social mobility, yet by different means. Jesus's method is in pushing the domineering envelope gradually while the mother of James and

---

4. Stephanie Buckhanon Crowder, "The Mother of James and John," *Just Women* 7, no. 2 (Spring 2015): 43.

John wants instant relief and power. There is no shame in her game of desperation. Let God's kingdom come, God's will be done . . . and get rid of the Roman kingdom. While you are at it, make sure my boys have a place on the throne! They are ready to play this kingdom game.

MRS. ZEBEDEE NOW

At any given sport events, it is not surprising to hear that a child say they wants to be the next superstar athlete. Boys yearn to be the one to dethrone "King James" LeBron or "Cam Newton." Serena and Venus Williams have girls watching their every move. While there is danger in mothers trying to live vicariously through their children, one cannot discount or discard the maternal drive to give children more. Of course, sports mothers can be scary, and the push can be too much. Thus there is the ubiquitous presence of behavioral guidelines and parental agreements.[5]

There is a unique sociology and a particular philosophy of mothers who spend hours and days at football practices, soccer games, tennis lessons, and basketball banquets. There is a "fearless" mindset of mothers whose lives revolve around ballet recitals and dance performances. For so many, ensuring their son's or daughter's future security is tantamount to their own well-being. These African American mothers do not play, if you will.

NBA star Kevin Durant provided a little insight into maternal machination and maneuvering. In 2014, Oklahoma City Thunder forward "KD" accepted the Most Valuable Player award.[6] During the speech KD thanked God and acknowledged friends and persons from his childhood community. Last, but not least, he tearfully thanked his family, especially his mother. Durant had this to say about her: "I don't think you know what you did. . . . You wake me up in the middle of the night in the summer times, making me run up a hill, making me do pushups, screaming at me from the sidelines of my games at 8 or 9 years old. . . . You the real MVP."[7]

Such raw emotions are not quantifiable. One cannot calculate what it takes to make a grown man cry on national television. Yet whatever

5. Brooke DeLench, "Talking to Your Child's Coach: Advice for Football Moms and Dads," http://www.momsteam.com/sports/talking-to-your-childs-coach-advice-for-football-moms-and-dads.

6. Kevin Durant, "MVP Speech" *The Oklahoman*, http://newsok.com/kevin-durant-the-oklahoma-city-thunder-stars-complete-mvp-speech/article/4815027.

7. Ibid.

it is, Wanda Pratt, Kevin Durant's mother, has it and has passed it on to her children. Apparently there was a benefit to all of her screaming and yelling. KD and his family no longer have to worry about moving from place to place or going to bed hungry. He will make over $200 million in 2016.[8]

Not all of the athletic yelling and sports histrionics lead to an NBA star, an NFL legacy, a tennis legend, or a golf green jacket. The numbers are scary. Only 3 percent of high school athletes will play college basketball, and a mere 1 percent will play professionally. The numbers for football are 6 percent and 2 percent respectively.[9] The numbers revealing African American ownership of sports teams is even more dismal. Magic Johnson owns a small percentage of the Los Angeles Lakers NBA Team. Bob Johnson used to own the Charlotte Bobcats before Michael Jordan bought the team and renamed it the Charlotte Hornets. Still, the name change did not add to the quantity of African American owners. We play on court and on the field, but we are not in the front office—period

Additionally, the body can only handle so much tackling, blocking, running, and pushing. Thus African American mothers, the ringleaders of this sociology of sports, must be honest with themselves and their children. They must instill a sense of academic excellence as well as athletic prowess.

Mothers who want their kids to have much more, be much better, and love God and God's people more may be able to empathize with the mother of James and John. They probably could understand her wanting the best for her boys. This mother took unorthodox measures to ensure a fruitful future for her sons. The means justified her desired end.

Felecia Jenkins also sheds light on the extent of maternal means. She taught her son, Kris, the basics of basketball, as she was a former player turned coach.[10] At an early age she involved him in AAU basketball leagues. She was so determined to give him a future of possibility, she decided to give Kris's AAU coach legal guardianship of her son. For the sake of his safety and in hope of better opportunities, this mother placed her son with another family.[11] In the end, Felecia Jenkins and

8. "Kevin Durant to Earn 200 million?", *Sports Illustrated Wire*. http://www.si.com/nba/2015/01/30/kevin-durant-thunder-200-million.

9. "Estimated Probability of Competing in Athletics beyond the High School Interscholastic Level," National Collegiate Athletic Association, http://www.ncaa.org/about/resources/research/probability-competing-beyond-high-school

10. Julia Jacobo, "Villanova's Kris Jenkins Credits His Mom for His Shooting Skills", *ABC News*, http://abcnews.go.com/US/villanovas-kris-jenkins-credits-mom-basketball-skills/story?id=38161375.

11. Roger Sherman, "The Incredible Story of Villanova's Kris Jenkins and UNC's Nate Britt," http://www

Kris won—literally. With less than a second on the clock, Kris Jenkins shot the game-winning three pointer that made Villanova the 2016 NCAA Basketball Champions. The world would know his name and ability. The world would also know the depth of his mother's sacrifice. These are the maternal "games" we play.

There are times when mothers must advocate and push systems and people on behalf of children. Better schools are a mandate. Well-trained teachers, principals, and social workers should not be exceptions to the rule. No, a police officer cannot just kill any black boy, or any person for that matter. Judicial accountability and civility are paramount. Like the mother of James and John, there are moments that not only push us to get on our knees and pray, but there are times we must also stand on our feet and march.

Yet a person does not have to be an African American mother, athlete, or sports fan to know about games. Human nature lends itself toward automatic game participation. We relish competition. We enjoy sport. We thrive on outperforming, outmaneuvering each other. We cannot help it. All of us may not don cleats, helmets, or the latest equipment. Nevertheless, life compels us to position ourselves with certain people. We diligently seek out and select specific universities, partners, and colleagues. We are discerning about whom we will date. One does not have to be an all-star, state-ranked athlete to play life's games. Let the ontological games begin.

The bottom line is honesty. Is the "ask" really about the children, or is it primarily about our unresolved issues? Is our "kingdom" language overshadowing what is really the essence of life—service to humankind?

Let's play!

Questions for Discussion

1. Discuss whether Mrs. Zebedee is asking too much of Jesus.
2. Why do you think James and John responded that they could handle the cup?
3. What types of "games" do you play?
4. Describe a time when your competitive nature got the best of you.
5. What does it mean to be "shameless"?

.sbnation.com/college-basketball/2016/4/3/11355344/villanova-north-carolina-adoptive-brothers-kris-jenkins
-nate-britt-national-championship-game.

PART THREE

Final Act

10

Where Do We Go from Here?

I rejoiced in them all, because wisdom leads them; but I did not know that she was their mother.

—book of Wisdom 7:12

Nine days after delivering her daughter, Marissa Alexander was in jail. While most mothers are adjusting to the joys of the birthing and newborns, Alexander was behind bars. This nightmare in 2010 began when her estranged husband entered their residence. Fearing for her life, Alexander fired a warning shot in the air. A jury rejected her "stand your ground" claim and sentenced her to twenty years. After taking a plea and agreeing to felony charges, this mother was finally released in January 2015. She served over one thousand days in jail, the majority of them absent from her infant child. Alexander will still have to serve under house arrest for two years.

One has to wonder if there is any word the Bible can offer a mother "standing" in Alexander's shoes. Readers often question the contextual relevance of the biblical text in general. Such interrogation becomes even more poignant when examining specific people living in certain times under unique social constructs. It is one thing for Christians and those who deem the Bible sacred to hold to its pertinence. A kind of generic, universal sociological approach to the biblical narrative is not uncommon. However, discovering and teasing out its relationship to more defined groups with a more specified social identity is quite a literary and practical undertaking.

This work has attempted to do just that. The purpose of the stories about biblical mothers falls on literary and socially deaf ears unless they mean something to twenty-first-century mothers. Meaning is subjective and not universal. It is as organic as the real flesh-and-blood readers themselves.[1] One mother's understanding from reading this book may be quite antipodal from another's understanding. Interpretation and social location pave the road from such interchange and unique praxis.

With that said, this work does not purport a one-size-fits-all path to interpretation. Whereas this project set out to define womanist maternal thought as the conversation race, gender, and class have with African American mothers, this is not the sum total. This is just the appetizer in hopes that others will come along and serve the main course and the dessert. Do not misunderstand—appetizers can be filling and satiating.

Lifting a hermeneutical lens under the auspices of womanist maternal thinking proposes to do just that: spur readers to think about ways that African American mothers engage literature. Although this research employed biblical narratives as its test cases, womanist maternal thought is applicable to other forms of literature. Such is especially possible since the idea of "womanism" did not emanate from the loins of biblical studies but from broader literary studies.

Much of this research examined the history, role, and plight of African American mothers. The point was to take the conversation beyond the Bible and demonstrate elements of the sociology of those who read it: in this case, mothers in the United States of African descent. Establishing a historical, social, and political grounding for African American mothers helps to paint a portrait of what shapes and molds these readers. Thus, understanding their identity in the past helps to shed light on how texts illuminate our present and can impact the future.

Through the framework of womanist biblical interpretation, this project laid a foundation examining race, class, and gender dynamics in the Bible. Whereas womanist thinking did not have its origin in the halls of biblical studies, its tenets lend themselves to examining how African American women come to read and see themselves in and through the Bible. From "womanist" thinkers like Jarena Lee, Elizabeth, and Anna Julia Cooper to current-day practitioners in the halls of the academy, African American female scholars and women who do not come from the loins of doctoral work continue to challenge racist, classist, and sexist ideology in the Bible and in those who interpret it.

A step beyond womanist biblical interpretation is the introduction of womanist maternal thought. This concept takes womanist thinking

---

1. Fernando F. Segovia, "And They Began to Speak in Other Tongues: Competing Modes of Discourse in Contemporary Biblical Criticism," in *Reading from This Place: Social Location and Biblical Interpretation in the United States*, vol. 1 (Minneapolis: Fortress Press, 1995), 31.

and couples it with womanist biblical hermeneutics to address motherhood. Such a novel framework provides a grounding for discussing how race, class, and gender impact the livelihood, progress, and state of African American mothers. Furthermore this method peruses mothers in the biblical text to glean what maternal messages are relevant to African American mothers now.

By beginning the discourse with the story of Hagar as mother, this work focuses on maternal displacement and what it means to be homeless. To value the story of Hagar and her surrogacy, one has to reimagine slave women raped and giving birth to the master's child. The story compels the audience to reconsider the duties of wet nursing and childrearing that enslaved women had to perform. Hagar's story of homelessness reconnects to the displacement slave women experienced.

Yet if the text is still relevant, then Hagar pulls us into the current day where African American women struggling with infertility find a path to motherhood through surrogacy. Furthermore, the homeless Hagar of the Bible should move readers today to act on behalf of women and their children in homeless shelters.

As knowledge of African American mothers and of their journeys is the root of this project, it helps to elucidate the struggles of Rizpah and her childless death watch. The class dynamic and imperial pressure that forced her to surrender her sons to hanging is not contextually obsolete. Mothers today still watch in agony as their children travel the school-to-prison pipeline. #Blacklivesmatter started from the cries of African American mothers who had to bury their children, like Rizpah.

Bathsheba reminds us that although African American mothers hold the bottom rung of the social ladder, they are still able to wield some power. It was not Bathsheba's sexual prowess but her rhetorical skill that secured the kingdom for her son. She was not "sceerred"; she was fearless. Bathsheba reminds the reader that baby mommas have to do what they do. This queen mother teaches African American mothers to handle their business and perform what is necessary for progeny security.

The stigma attached to teen mothers could be abated through examination of Mary, the mother of Jesus, as a teen mother. The mother of the Savior of the world was just a teen, maybe a preteen when Gabriel proclaimed her as "favored," not favorless. No one is encouraging an adolescent to partake in adult responsibilities. God still used Mary's status as a teenage girl living in a male dominated society to bring salvation into the world. Her gender and class did not preclude her divine assignment. However, the care that Elizabeth gave to a young Mary is the same attention and affection young mothers need from wise mothers today. This sense of communal mothering has been a part of the African and African American motherhood fabric. There has always been a Mary-Elizabeth approach to mothering. Our children benefit from these relationships.

Twenty-first-century mothers learn from the Canaanite mother that sometimes we get called out of our names for the sake of our children's well-being. Nonetheless, this mother was relentless. She worked her words and verbally best-ed Jesus. The mother had a faith that would not quit. Her advocacy for her daughter's well-being is a model of the efforts African American mothers must take for our children's wholeness and well-being.

I have learned of the idiosyncratic tendencies of sports moms. We are shameless in what we do, even to the point of questioning coaches. The mother of James and John, Mrs. Zebedee, was just as bold in her request. She played the kingdom game and sought prime seats for her sons. If nothing else, mothers can take cues from her in how to play the games of life. Mothers must check the reason for the request and have a fair assessment of their children's abilities. Yet we must be sure not to disqualify ourselves or our children. There is a cup to bear.

Womanist maternal thinking as the intersection of gender construction, class dynamics, and race revelation through the eyes of African American mothers helps the reader to see the aforementioned biblical narratives differently. Other methods could yield similar or different results. However, as an African American mother and a student of the tripartite grid of race-class-gender, this approach to interpretation rests with me and moves me.

Although this research offers distinct views of these biblical mothers, there are still more trajectories and points of further investigation. First, the academy has to address nuances of motherhood and parenting. I was intrigued to see Melissa Harris-Perry offering a course on the politics of motherhood. What impressed me more was her course description and purpose:

> . . . to discuss the relevance of parental identity in the political choices of women; the cultural and political battles surrounding reproductive justice and the ability of women to choose motherhood; . . . motherhood . . . in popular culture; and the intersections of race, class and sexual orientation with the politics of motherhood.[2]

2. Melissa Harris-Perry, Politics of Motherhood, course syllabus, http://cooperproject.org/mhp-syllabi/.

"Race, class and sexual orientation . . . motherhood" sounds like womanist maternal thought to me. It is important to discuss and evaluate the power of motherhood. Organizations such as Moms Demand Action are harnessing the maternal might to fight gun violence. There is indeed a motherhood movement that warrants study.

As a 2015 Supreme Court ruling has made same-sex marriage a right, the presence of LGBTQ mothering is another necessary conversation partner. In addition the language of fathers who are mothering is worthy of exploration. There are men who by choice or by force are serving in both roles. Some mothers have forfeited their duties. Some mothers are in prison. A biblical perspective on mother-fathers is fertile ground.

Furthermore, wider interreligious dialogue around mothering and motherhood will only add to the knowledge and information base. An examination of commonalities and distinctions emanating from various religious groups is an automatic trajectory. This could help to expose persons to distinct religious perspectives and how family dynamics reflect said traditions.

A dialogue among mothers of various racial and ethnic backgrounds is due. There are indeed distinct nuances to being an African American mother. Yet "tiger mom" moves and motives can be universal. It is integral to the broader maternal conversation that experiences, activity, and lessons across cultural boundaries come to the surface.

Continued research on intergenerational approaches to motherhood and communal mothering is still paramount as the age for mothers and grandmothers is getting younger. The Mary-Elizabeth connection with a twenty-first-century twist provides a means for truth telling and wisdom dissemination.

There were mothers that this research did not include. As stated earlier, the six selected were initially sermon topics. It appears that I have more preaching to do: for example, Eve, Gomer, the mother of 2 Maccabees 7, Peter's mother-in-law, and the Mother Whore of Revelation to name a few. There is much to draw from these and other maternal literary waters.

Ultimately the hope is that this book will encourage readers to not only pay attention to the way the biblical texts portray motherhood, but also to scrutinize society's present treatment of mothers. Lifting homeless, shameless, fearless biblical characters must propel readers to do something about homelessness and to consider shameless and fearless acts that support motherhood and undergird children. As I was writing, my heart was flooded with thoughts of Ebony Wilkerson, Zakieya

Avery, Leatrice Brewer, Miriam Carey, Susan Smith, and the countless
mothers whose momentary weakness was not indicative of their overall
strength.[3] Maybe it is not for us to understand why mothers kill their
children or put them in harm's way. They are still mothers.

Discussing what it means to lack favor, to be childless and yet relentless, should propel us to connect with whatever mental, physical, and
internal challenges hinder personal fulfillment and impede our own
maternal drive. In the end, whether in the church, academy, or public
square, may this work assuage, stir, move, disturb, and conscript us to
know the source of our own strength.

Know and access the power of the maternal voice—something happens when Momma speaks!!

Questions for Discussion

1. What in the nature of motherhood is universal to all mothers?
2. What advice would you like to offer mothers?
3. Which of the six biblical mothers most speaks to your understanding of motherhood? Why?
4. Describe a nonbiblical mother who serves as a model for you.
5. How would you finish the following: When I speak . . . ?

3. "Mom Ebony Wilkerson, Who Drove Kids into Ocean, Is Ordered Committed," *NBC News*, December 23,
2014, http://www.nbcnews.com/news/us-news/mom-ebony-wilkerson-who-drove-kids-ocean-ordered
-committed-n273706; Carol Kuruvilla, "Maryland Women Accused of Killing Children Were Part of 'Demon
Assassin' Exorcism Cult," *Daily News*, January 23, 2014, http://www.nydailynews.com/news/crime/exorcism
-killers-part-demon-assassin-cult-article-1.1589520; Teresa L. Fry Brown, "Leatrice Brewer Update: Judge Says
N.Y. Mother Who Killed Her Children is Not Entitled to Piece of Their Estate," *CBS News*, November 6, 2013,
http://www.cbsnews
.com/news/leatrice-brewer-update-judge-says-ny-mother-who-killed-her-children-is-not-entitled-to-piece-of-their
-estate/; Steven Almsy, "Woman Killed during D.C. Chase Was Shot Five Times from Behind, Autopsy Shows,"
CNN, April 10, 2014, http://www.cnn.com/2014/04/08/us/miriam-carey-autopsy/; Eun Kyung Kim, "Susan
Smith Tells Reporter She Is Not a 'Monster' 20 Years after Conviction for Killing Sons," *Today News*, July 23,
2015, http://www.today.com/news/susan-smith-tells-reporter-she-not-monster-20-years-after-t34081.

Selected Bibliography

Ahmad, Farah. "How Women of Color Are Driving Entrepreneur-ship." The Center for American Progress. https://www .americanprogress.org/issues/race/report/2014/06/10/91241/how -women-of-color-are-driving-entrepreneurship/.

Alexander, Michelle. *The New Jim Crow: Mass Incarceration in the Age of Colorblindness.* New York: New Press, 2012.

Almasy, Steve. "Woman Killed during D.C. Chase Was Shot Five Times from Behind, Autopsy Shows." *CNN News.* http://www.cnn .com/2014/04/08/us/miriam-carey-autopsy/.

Anderson, Cheryl. *Ancient Laws and Contemporary Controversies: The Need for Inclusive Interpretation.* New York: Oxford University Press, 2009.

Bridgeman, Valerie. "The Inspiration of Rizpah's Courageous Help-lessness." In *Global Perspectives on the Bible,* edited by Mark Ron-cace and Joseph Weaver, 105–6. Boston: Pearson Education, 2014.

Brown, Teresa L. Fry. *God Don't Like Ugly: African American Women Handing on Spiritual Values.* Nashville: Abingdon Press, 2000.

———. "Leatrice Brewer Update: Judge Says N.Y. Mother Who Killed Her Children Is Not Entitled to Piece of Their Estate." *CBS News.* http://www.cbsnews.com/news/leatrice- brewer-update -judge-says-ny-mother-who-killed-her-children-is-not-entitled-to -piece-of-their-estate/.

Casey, Timothy. "Single Mother Snapshot." Legal Momentum. http://www.legalmomentum.org/sites/default/files/reports/single -mothers-snapshot_0.pdf.

Centers for Disease Control and Prevention. "Births: Final Data for 2012." http://www.cdc.gov/nchs/data/nvsr/nvsr62/nvsr62_09 .pdf#table06.

Chicago Tribune Wire Reports via Associated Press. "Almost Half of U.S. Households Exhaust Their Salaries." *Chicago Tribune.* http:// www.chicagotribune.com/business/breaking/chi-households -exhaust-salaries-20150129-story.html.

Children's Defense Fund. http://www.childrensdefense.org/.

Coates, Ta-Nehisi. "Understanding Out-of-Wedlock Births in Black America." *The Atlantic*. http://www.theatlantic.com/sexes/archive/2013/06/understanding-out-of-wedlock-births-in-black-america/277084/.

Coleman, Monica. *Ain't I a Womanist Too? Third-Wave Womanist Religious Thought*. Minneapolis: Fortress Press, 2013.

———. *"Making A Way Out of No Way: A Womanist Theology*. Minneapolis: Fortress Press, 2008.

Collins, Patricia Hill. *Black Feminist Thought: Knowledge, Consciousness, and the Politics of Empowerment*. 2nd ed. New York: Routledge, 2000.

Crowder, Stephanie Buckhanon. "Biblical/Black Mother Working/Wrecking," *Semeia Studies* 61 (November 2009): 157–67.

———. *"Simon of Cyrene: A Case of Roman Conscription*. New York: Peter Lang, 2002.

———. "Mary: The Mother of Jesus." *Just Women* 7, no. 2. (Spring 2015): 26–31.

———. "The Canaanite Woman." *Just Women* 7, no. 2 (Spring 2015): 32–37.

———. "The Mother of James and John." *Just Women* 7, no. 2 (Spring 2015): 40–44.

DeLench, Brooke. "Talking to Your Child's Coach: Advice for Football Moms and Dads." http://www.momsteam.com/sports/talking-to-your-childs-coach-advice-for-football-moms-and-dads.

Dickerson, Bette. *African American Single Mothers: Understanding Their Lives and Families*. Thousand Oaks, CA: SAGE Publications, 1995.

Dixon, Patricia. *African American Relationships, Marriages, and Families: An Introduction*. New York: Routledge, 2007.

Douglas, Kelly Brown. "Marginalized People, Liberating Perspectives: A Womanist Approach to Biblical Interpretation." *Anglican Theological Review* 83, no 1 (2001): 41–48.

DuBois, W. E. B. *The Gift of Black Folk: Negroes in the Making of America*. New York: Square One Publishers, 2009.

Durant, Kevin. "MVP Speech." *The Oklahoman*. http:// newsok.com/kevin-durant-the-oklahoma-city-thunder-stars-complete-mvp-speech/article/4815027.

Dutton, Zoie. "Abortion's Racial Gap." *The Atlantic*. http://www.theatlantic.com/health/archive/2014/09/abortions-racial-gap/380251/.

Edelman, Marian Wright. "A Prayer for Our Children." In *Guide My Feet*, 102–10. Boston: Beacon Press, 2013.

Ehrman, Bart D. *A Brief Introduction to the New Testament*. 2nd ed. New York: Oxford University Press, 2009.

Elizabeth. "Elizabeth: A Colored Minister of the Gospel, Born in Slavery." In *Black Women in Nineteenth-Century American Life*, edited by Bert Lowenberg and Ruth Bogin, 127–34. University Park: Pennsylvania State University Press, 1991.

Essex, Barbara J. "Some Kind of Woman: The Making of a Strong Black Woman." In *Embracing the Spirit: Womanist Perspectives on Hope, Salvation and Transformation*, 203–11. Maryknoll, NY: Orbis Books, 1997.

Exum, Cheryl. "Rizpah." In *Women in Scripture*, edited by Carol Myers, 145–46. Grand Rapids: Eerdmans, 2000.

———. "Rizpah," in *Word and World* 17 (1997): 260–68.

Felder, Cain Hope, ed. *Stony the Road We Trod: African American Biblical Interpretation*. Minneapolis: Fortress Press, 1991.

"Fertility for Colored Girls." http://www.fertilityforcoloredgirls.org/#!projects/c21kz.

Frazier, E. Franklin. *The Negro Family in the United States*. Chicago: University of Chicago Press, 1968.

Fung, Katherine. "The Surrogacy Journey She Took for Her Daughter." *The Huffington Post*. http://www.huffingtonpost.com/2014/02/18/melissa-harris-perry-baby-surrogacy-ivf_n_4808049.html.

Gafney, Wilda. "Translation Matters: A Fem/Womanist Exploration of Translation Theory and Practice for Proclamation in Worship." SBL Forum. http://www.sbl-site.org/assets/pdfs/gafney.pdf.

Garroway, Kristine. "Was Bathsheba the Original Bridget Jones?" *Nashim: Journal of Jewish Women's Studies* 24 (2013): 53–73.

Giddings, Paula. *When and Where I Enter: The Impact of Black Women on Race and Sex in America*. New York: Morrow, 1984.

Gilkes, Cheryl Townsend. *If It Wasn't for the Women*. Maryknoll, NY: Orbis, 2001.

Haimerl, Amy. " The Fastest Growing Group of Entrepreneurs in America." http://fortune.com/2015/06/29/black-women-entrepreneurs/.

Harris-Perry, Melissa. The Politics of Motherhood. Course syllabus. http://cooperproject.org/mhp-syllabi/.

Hurston, Zora Neale. *Dust Tracks on the Road*. New York, NY: Harper Collins, 1942.

Jacobo, Julia. "Villanova's Kris Jenkins Credits His Mom for His Shooting Skills." http://abcnews.go.com/US/villanovas-kris-jenkins-credits-mom-basketball-skills/story?id=38161375.

Jacobs, Mignon. "Mothering a Leader: Bathsheba's Relational and Functional Identities." In *Mother Goose, Mother Jones, Mommie Dearest: Biblical Mothers and Their Children*, edited by Cheryl A. Kirk-Duggan and Tina Pippin, 67–84. Atlanta: Society of Biblical Literature, 2009.

Jones-Warsaw, Koala. "Toward a Womanist Hermeneutic: A Reading of Judges 19–21." *Journal of the Interdenominational Theological Center* 22 (1994): 18–35.

Kim, Eun Kyung. "Susan Smith Tells Reporter She Is Not a 'Monster' 20 Years after Conviction for Killing Sons." *Today News.* http://www.today.com/news/susan-smith-tells-reporter-she-not-monster-20-years-after-t34081.

King, Karen. "Women in Ancient Christianity." *Frontline: From Jesus to Christ.* http://www.pbs.org/wgbh/pages/frontline/shows/religion/first/ women.html.

Kuruvilla, Carol. "Maryland Women Accused of Killing Children Were Part of 'Demon Assassin' Exorcism Cult. *Daily News.* http://www.nydailynews.com/news/crime/exorcism-killers-part-demon-assassin-cult-article-1.1589520.

Kwoh, Leslie. "Xerox CEO Ursula Burns Has Advice for Ambitious Women." *Wall Street Journal.* March, 20, 2013. http://blogs.wsj.com/atwork/2013/03/20/xerox-ceo-ursula-burns-has-advice-for-ambitious-women/.

Lee, Jarena. "Religious Experience and Journal of Mrs. Jarena Lee, Giving an Account of Her Call to Preach the Gospel. In *Black Women in Nineteenth-Century American Life*, edited by Bert Lowenberg and Ruth Bogin, 135–41. University Park: Pennsylvania State University Press, 1991.

Lewis, Shawn D. "Family Planning's Top Advocate." *Ebony Magazine.* September 1978. https://books.google.com/books?id=TM0DAAAAMBAJ.

Mitchem, Stephanie. *Womanist Theology.* Maryknoll, NY: Orbis Books, 2002.

"Mom Ebony Wilkerson, Who Drove Kids into Ocean, Is Ordered Committed. *NBC News.* http://www.nbcnews.com/news/us-news/mom-ebony-wilkerson-who-drove-kids-ocean-ordered-committed-n273706.

Moynihan, Patrick. "The Tangle of Pathology." http://www.dol.gov /dol/aboutdo/history/moynchapter4.htm.

National Association for Children of Alcoholics. http:// www.nacoa .net/pdfs/addicted.pdf.

National Coalition for the Homeless. http://www.nationalhomeless .org/factsheets/families.html.

National Collegiate Athletic Association. "Estimated Probability of Competing in Athletics beyond the High School Interscholastic Level." http://www.ncaa.org/about/resources/research/probability -competing-beyond-high-school.

Newsom, Carol, and Sharon Ringe, eds. *Women's Bible Commentary*. 3rd ed. Louisville, KY: Westminster John Knox Press, 2012.

Northup, Solomon. *Twelve Years a Slave*. London: Sampson Low and Company, 1853.

Patte, Daniel. *The Global Bible Commentary*. Nashville: Abingdon Press, 2004.

Schneider, Tammi J. *Mothers of Promise: Women in the Book of Genesis*. Grand Rapids: Baker Books, 2008.

Sharp, Diamond. "Black Mothers under Siege." *The Root*. http:// www.theroot.com/photos/2014/08/black_mothers_under_siege .html.

Sherman, Roger. "The Incredible Story of Villanova's Kris Jenkins and UNC's Nate Britt." http://www.sbnation.com/college-basketball /2016/4/3/11355344/villanova-north- carolina-adoptive-brothers -kris-jenkins-nate-britt-national-championship-game.

The Shriver Report. *A Woman's Nation Pushes Back from the Brink*. http://shriverreport.org/a-womans-nation-pushes-back-from-the -brink-facts-and-figures/.

Smith, Mitzi. "Knowing More Than Is Good for One." In *Teaching All the Nations: Interrogating the Matthean Great Commission*, edited by Mitzi J. Smith and Jayachitra Lalitha, 127–58. Minneapolis: Fortress Press, 2014.

Smith, Shanell T. *The Woman Babylon and the Marks of Empire: Reading Revelation with a Postcolonial Womanist Hermeneutics of Ambiveilence*. Minneapolis: Fortress Press, 2014.

Spink-Palmieri, Sheri. "Working vs Staying Home Mothers." *Baby Talk* 71. no. 7 (September 2006): 54–56.

Sports Illustrated Wire. "Kevin Durant to Earn 200 Million on Next Contract?" http://www.si.com/nba/2015/01/30/kevin-durant-thunder -200-million.

St. Clair, Rachel. "Womanist Biblical Interpretation." In *True to Our Native Land: An African American New Testament Commentary*, edited by Brian Blount, 54–62. Minneapolis: Fortress Press, 2007.

Stephens, Rhiannon. *A History of African Motherhood: The Case of Uganda 700–1900*. New York: Cambridge University Press, 2013.

Stewart, Maria W. "Maria Stewart." In *Black Women in Nineteenth-Century American Life*, edited by Bert Lowenberg and Ruth Bogin, 183-200. University Park: Pennsylvania State University Press, 1991.

Sudarkasa, Niara. *The Strength of Our Mothers: African and African American Women and Families*. Trenton: African World Press, 1996.

Thurman, Howard. *Jesus and the Disinherited*. Boston: Beacon Press, 1976.

The Trayvon Martin Foundation. http://www.trayvonmartinfoundation .org.

U.S. Census Bureau. Table C3. "Living Arrangements of Children Under 18 Years and Marital Status of Parents, by Age, Sex, Race, and Hispanic Origin and Selected Characteristics of the Child for All Children: 2010." http://www.census.gov/population/www /socdemo/hh-fam/cps2010.html.

U. S. Department of Health and Human Services. Office of Adolescent Health. "Trends in Teen Pregnancy and Childbirth." http:// www.hhs.gov/ash/oah/adolescent-health-topics/reproductive -health/teen-pregnancy/trends.html#.U6ygsSjxp74.

———. "Dad Stats." http://www.fatherhood.gov/library/dad-stats.

Walker, Alice. *In Search of Our Mothers' Gardens: Womanist Prose*. Orlando: Harcourt Inc., 1983.

Walker-Barnes, Chanequa. *Too Heavy a Yoke: Black Women and the Burden of Strength*. Eugene, OR: Cascade Books, 2014.

Washington, Jesse. "Blacks Struggle with 72 Percent Unwed Mothers Rate." November 7, 2010. http://www.nbcnews.com/id/39993685 /ns/health-womens_health/t/blacksstruggle-unwed-mothers-rate /#.VMmBAsZOpm1.

Weekly, Heather. "Q and A: Sam's Club's Rosalind Brewer." *Capital Style*. January/February 2014. http://www.capital-style.com /content/stories/2014/01/business-savvy.html.

Weems, Renita J. "My Mother, My Self." In *Showing Mary: How*

Women Can Share Prayers, Wisdom, and the Blessings of God, 117-25. West Bloomfield, MI: Walk Worthy Press, 2002.

————. "African American Women and the Bible." In *Stony the Road We Trod: African American Biblical Interpretation,* edited by Cain Hope Felder, 57–80. Minneapolis: Fortress Press, 1991.

Williams, Delores S. *Sisters in the Wilderness: The Challenge of Womanist God-Talk.* New York: Orbis Books, 1993.

Index

Abishag, 65, 67
abortion, 60, 70
Abraham, 41–51, 86
action, faith and, 84–91
activism
  community mothers and, 13–14
  not allowing societal/class status to
    limit, 30–31
  political, 10, 30
  women who engage institutional powers
    for the good of children, xv, 84–91
addiction, 12, 61, 68
Adonijah, 64–67, 71
advocacy, xiv
  on behalf of children, xv, 84–91, 101,
    108
  motherhood as, xiv
  those with power as needing to advocate
    for others on the margins, 14, 82
  as work, 27, 89, 91
Africa
  family structures in, 5–6
  motherhood in, xiii
  West African tribes/cultures, 5–7, 15
African American Codes, 24
African American families, 10–11, 22n13,
  84–85
African American men
  and incarceration, 59
  and income/economic disparities, 10
  leading cause of death for, 58
African American mothers, 3–16, 22
  class distinctions among, 26
  and single motherhood, 79–80
  socioeconomic status of, 48, 107
  teen birth rates among, 12, 81
  and womanist maternal thought, xiii–
    xiv, 17–27

  work for, 23–27
  See also specific topics/descriptions, e.g.,
    "other mothering"
African American people, 21–22, 58–60,
  69–70
African American women
  in the corporate world, 9
  experiences of, 19–20
  feminism, as challenging, 21
  in professional and managerial
    positions, xiii, 48
  and the right to decide about
    motherhood, 70, 108
  on social/class ladder, 82
  work for, 23–27
  See also intersection of race, gender,
    sexuality, and class; womanism;
    specific topics, e.g., stereotypes
"African American Women and the Bible"
  (Weems), 33
African diaspora, xiii, 19
African Methodist Episcopal church,
  30–31
Ahmad, Farah, 68
Alabama, 13
alcohol abuse, 60–61
Alexander, Marissa, 105
"also a mother" language, 24, 69, 89
"ambiveilence," 34–35
Anderson, Tanisha, 58
Angelou, Maya, 17
antebellum era, 49–50
Apocalypse of John. *See* Revelation, book of
Asian American women
  percent of children born to single
    mothers, 79
  in professional and managerial
    positions, xiii, 48

asthma, 60–61
authority
    mother-centered, 9
    See also power; *specific topics/descriptions,*
        e.g., patriarchy
Avery, Zakieya, 109–10

Babylon, whore of, 34
Babylonian exile, 29
"baby mommas," xiii, 43, 60, 79, 107
Baker, Ella, 13, 20
Banks, Tyra, 3
baptism, 35
Baptists, 14
barrenness
    of Sarah, 41–51
    See also infertility
basic needs, 26, 59
Bassett, Angela, 3
Bathsheba, 96
    as fearless mother, xv, 63–72, 107
beauty, 75
Being Mary Jane (television show), 49
Berry, Halle, 3, 79–80
Bethune, Mary MacLeod, 14, 27
Beyoncé, 3
Bible, 105–10
    the Great Commission, 35
    Pentateuch, four versions of (J, E, D,
        and P), 42n5
    universal sociological approach to, 105
    womanist hermeneutics/interpretation,
        xiv, 19, 21, 28–37, 106–7
    See also New Testament; Old
        Testament
biblical mothers, xiv. *See individual names,*
        e.g., Hagar; Mary the mother of
        Jesus; Rizpah
birth control, 12, 70
Black Lives Matter, 107
Black women
    experiences of, 19–20
    See also African American women
Bland, Sandra
bleeding woman, 87
bloodlines, 5–6
Brady Bunch, The (sitcom), 3

breadwinners, 4, 10
Brewer, Leatrice, 110
Brewer, Rosalind, 69–72
Brown, Bobbi Kristina, 68
Brown, Michael, 52–53, 58
Brown, Teresa L. Fry, 22
Burns, Ursula, 69–72
Burroughs, Nannie Helen, 14
business. *See topics beginning with "job"*; work

calling, 26
    a woman's call to preach, 30–31, 36
camp, 4
Canaanite woman, xv, 108
    as relentless mother, 84–91
capitalism, 10, 15, 97
    and exploitation, 7
career, xii–xiii, 25
    family and, xiii, 22, 69, 90–91
    See also work
Carey, Miriam, 110
Caucasian American women
    percent of children born to single
        mothers, 79
    in professional and managerial
        positions, xiii, 48
    teen birth rates among, 81
    and unintended pregnancy, 60
"character building," 4–5
chattel slavery. *See* slavery
childcare, xiii, 11, 85. *See also* daycare
childlessness, 49
    Rizpah as childless mother, 52–62
    Sarah's barrenness, 41–51
children
    child poverty, 80
    close bond between African American
        mothers and, 24
    mothers living vicariously through, xv,
        92–101
    women who engage institutional powers
        for the good of, xv, 84–91
    See also specific topics, e.g., school
Children's Defense Fund (CDF), 88–89
Christology, 8
church mothers, 13–16
Church of God in Christ (denomination), 14

cigarette smoke, secondhand, 60–61
Circle of Mothers Empowerment Retreat, 52
circumcision, 43
citizenship, 7
Civil Rights Movement, xiii, 20, 89
Civil War, 28
Clark, Septima, 20
class, 18–19, 84
    class consciousness, 30, 32
    class distinctions, 26, 79, 82
    classism, 18, 21, 27, 77, 82, 88, 91, 106
    feminist movement and, 20
    middle class, 48, 84–85
    the one percent, 84
    prejudice, 14
    social mobility, xv, 98
    socioeconomic status, 12, 48
    and womanist maternal thought, 17–27
    See also intersection of race, gender,
        sexuality, and class; *specific topics and*
        individual names, e.g., Bathsheba;
        Hagar; Rizpah
Codes, African American, 24
Codes, Household. *See* Household Codes
Coleman, Monica, 20–21, 26
Collins, Patricia Hill, 10, 23–24, 58, 85
colonization, 87
common sense, 14
community
    communal mothering, 7, 49, 57, 108–9
    community mothers, 13–16, 27
    community programs, 91
    triple consciousness of family, work,
        and community, 24, 82
competition, 101
concubines, 65, 67
    Rizpah as, 52–62
conjugality, 5
consanguinity, 5–6
contraception, 12, 70
Cooper, Anna Julia, 20, 29, 106
Cotton, Dorothy, 20
courage, 19. *See also* fearlessness
covenants
    divine, 43
    imperative to covenant with another
        woman, 83

Craigslist ad seeking shelter, 17–18
criminal activity, 47, 59
criminal justice system, 59, 101
    inequalities in, 58
    juries lacking people of color, 58
    See also prison
Crowder, Stephanie Buckhanon, 34n24,
    52, 92
crucifixion, 93, 96
culture
    black women's, 19
    dominant, 19, 27
current-day mothers, xvi, 69

Darden, Gloria, 53
David
    Bathsheba and, xv, 63–72, 96
    Jesus as "Son of," 87–88
    Joseph as from line of, 75–76
    Rizpah and, xiv, 52–62
    seventeen sons of, 65
Davis, Jordan, 58
daycare, 25, 47, 68, 90
death
    African American men, leading cause of
        death for, 58
    early, of children, xiv, 52–62
    of Jesus, foretold, 92–101
    social, 59
    See also homicide
demon-possession, 84–91
dialogue
    among mothers of various racial and
        ethnic backgrounds, 109
    interreligious, 109
Dickerson, Bette, 81, 84–85
discipleship, 34
disciples of Jesus, 31, 84–101
    as fishermen, 97
discrimination, racial, 14
Dixon, Patricia, 9
dog, Canaanite woman called, 86–87
domestic violence, 60–61
domestic work, 8, 57
dominance, 11
dominant culture, 19, 27
double consciousness, xiii

drugs
  addiction, 12, 63, 68
  bad drug deals, 58
  epidemic of, 80
  mothers with children on, xiv
  use/abuse, 59–61, 63
Dube, Musa W., 87
DuBois, W. E. B., 8
Durant, Kevin, 99–100
Dutton, Zoie, 60

economics, 20, 58–59
  African American men and economic
    disparities, 10
  crash of 2008, 84
  exploitation, 7–8, 18
  freedom, 23, 26
  oppression, 46
  poverty and, 80
  See also financial stability/instability;
    specific topics, e.g., middle class
Edelman, Marian Wright, 84, 89
education, 14
  and academic excellence, 100
  African American mothers and,
    100
  for African American women, 14
  athletes and, 100
  Christian, 14
  and common sense, 14
  and the job market, 59
  training in the home, 4
  See also school
Egypt (Hagar as Egyptian), 41–51
Elijah, 95
Elizabeth (Mary's cousin), 76, 78–79,
  81–83, 107–9
Elizabeth (minister of the Gospel), 29,
  31–32, 36, 106
Emancipation Proclamation, 50
employment. See topics beginning with
  "job"; work
enslavement. See under slavery:
  enslavement
entrepreneurship, 68–69, 97
equality, 20, 44
Essex, Barbara J., 22
Esther, 30

ethnic groups/ethnicity, xvi, 21, 26, 37,
  46, 59, 87, 90
  dialogue among mothers of various
    racial and ethnic backgrounds, 109
Eve, 109
Exodus, book of, 29, 78
exploitation, economic, 7–8, 18
extended family, 6, 11–13
Exum, Cheryl, 55–56

faith, 46
  African American women's
    understanding of, xiv
  the Canaanite woman's, 84–91
  womanist biblical interpretation, 28–37
faith-based initiatives, 91
family, 11
  African American, 10–11, 22n13, 84–85
  career and, xiii, 22, 69, 90–91
  consanguinity and conjugality, 5–6
  extended, 6, 11–13
  the term, 11
  triple consciousness of family, work,
    and community, 24, 82
  See also specific topics/descriptions, e.g.,
    matrifocal families; West African
    tribes/cultures
family leave, 91
family structure
  African, 5
  structures of slavery and, 15
  and teen/adolescent births, 12–13
famine, 53–54, 56
Fassbender, Michael, 41–42
fathers
  single, 4
  stay-at-home, 4
  who are mothering, 109
favor (Mary as favor[less] mother), 73–83
fearlessness (Bathsheba as fearless mother),
  xv, 63–72, 107
feminism
  African American women as
    challenging, 21
  feminist maternal theology, xiv
  feminist movement in the United
    States, 20
  feminist theologians, 20

womanism and, 19–21, 33–35
Ferguson, Missouri, 58
fertility, 49. *See also* infertility
Fertility for Colored Girls, 49
financial crisis of 2008, 84
financial stability/instability, xv, 18, 26, 48, 59, 80–82
1 Kings, book of, 63–72
fishermen, 97
food insecurity, 79–80
food stamps, 79
foreigners, 78, 87
foresight, 71
Fortune 500 companies, 68–72
foster care, 12
Frazier, E. Franklin, 5–6, 41
Frazier-Herskovits Debate, 5–6
freedom, 14, 19, 23, 26, 77
Freedom Summer, 13
Fulton, Sybrina, 52, 61
future, xvi, 70–71, 105–10

Gabriel, 73–83, 107
Gafney, Wilda, 32–33
games, 92–101
gangs, xiv, 53, 58, 60
Garden of Gethsemane, 95
Gardner, Eric, 58
gender, 18–19
    dynamics, 30, 36, 56, 106
    and womanist maternal thought, 17–27
    See also intersection of race, gender, sexuality, and class; *specific topics/ descriptions,* e.g., patriarchy
Genesis, book of, 41–51
Gethsemane, Garden of, 95
ghetto, 82
Gibeonites, 52–62
Gilkes, Cheryl Townsend, 14–15
"Giving an Account of Her Call to Preach the Gospel" (Lee), 30–31
God
    Abram-Sarai-Hagar and, 41–51
    and Mary the mother of Jesus, xv, 73–83
    plans of, 81
godmothers, xiii
God-talk, xiv
Gomer, 109

Good Times (sitcom), 3
gossip, avoiding, 83
government
    social policies, 10
    and systemic decay, 54
    See also politics; *specific topics/ descriptions,* e.g., Roman Empire
graduation, xiii, 80
grandmothers, xiii, 12, 22n13, 81, 91, 109
Gray, Freddie, 53
Great Commission, 35
greatness, true, 94, 101
greed, 98
grief, a mother's, 52–62, 107
guilt trips, 69
gun violence, 52–53, 109

Hagar, 33, 41–51, 107
    power of, 44–45
    surrogacy of, xiv, 41–51, 107
"Hagar and Her Children" (Frazier), 41
Hamer, Fannie Lou, 13, 20
Hannah, 78
Hansberry, Lorraine, 11
Harper, Frances Ellen Watkins, 3–5, 29
Harris-Perry, Melissa, 49, 108–9
hatred, xvii, 83
"Haustafeln (Household Codes) in African American Biblical Interpretation: 'Free Slaves' and 'Subordinate Women'" (Martin), 33
healing, 24
    of the Canaanite woman's child, 84–91
health insurance, 80
Hebrew Bible. *See* Old Testament
Height, Dorothy, 14
Herod, King, 97
Herod Antipas, 97
Herodias, 87–88, 95
Herskovits, Melville Jean, 5–6
Hispanic American women
    female professionals, xiii
    per cent of children born to single mothers, 79
    teen birth rates among, 12, 81
Hispanic American women (*cont.*)
    and unintended pregnancy, 60
Holy Spirit, 78

home, 47
    training in, 4
    See also households
homelessness, 47–50
    Craigslist ad seeking shelter, 17–18
    Hagar as homeless mother, 41–51
    homeless shelters, xiv, 18, 47–48, 107
    job security and, 47
homicide, 52–62, 110
honesty, 101
hope, 46
Household Codes, 33
households, 6, 11, 81
    two-parent, 4, 84
    See also family; *specific topics/descriptions,*
        e.g., single parents
housing market debacle, 84
Houston, Whitney, 63–64, 68
humanity, 7, 94–95
    greatness as coming from service to,
        94, 101
    human nature, 95, 101
human rights, 14
humility, 98
Hurston, Zora Neale, 73

imperialism/imperialistic activity, 35, 75, 95
incarceration. *See* prison
income. *See* wages/income
individualism, 7
inequality, 58, 77
inequity, 18, 75
infertility, 49, 107
injustice, xvii, 30, 55
    confronting, 37
In Search of Our Mothers' Gardens
        (Walker), xii
insecurity, personal, xv, 75
intersection of race, gender, sexuality, and
        class, 7, 18–19, 22–23, 30–32, 34, 108
    race-class-gender triad, 36, 106, 108
intervention, 89
in vitro fertilization, 49
Isaac, 43, 86
Ish-bosheth or Ishbaal (Saul's son), 55
Ishmael, 43–44, 46
Israel, 52–72, 76, 86, 88

Jacob, 86
Jacobs, Mignon, 66
jail. *See* prison
James and John, 95. *See also* Zebedee's wife
Jenkins, Felicia, 100–101
Jenkins, Kris, 100–101
Jeremiah, book of, 29
Jerusalem, 93
Jesus, xv
    the Canaanite woman and, 84–91, 108
    death of, as foretelling, 92–101
    as Jew, 86
    Mary the mother of, xv, 73–83
    Matthean genealogy of, 86
    Matthew's, 95
    mother of James and John (Zebedee's
        wife) and, xv, 92–101
    resurrection of, 96
Jews, 26, 30, 74, 76, 98
    Jesus as, 86
    Mary as, 77
    in the Roman Empire, 77
job interviews
    children in the car during, 17
    "off the record" questions at, xiii, 91
joblessness, 80, 84
job market
    education and, 59
    and men released from prison, 59–60
job security, 47, 59
John, Apocalypse of. *See* Revelation, book of
John, James and, 95. *See also* Zebedee's wife
Johnson, Bob, 100
Johnson, Magic, 100
Jonathan, 54, 56
Jordan, Michael, 100
Joseph, 73–83
Judah, 86, 93
Junior, Nyasha, 32–33, 35–36
juries lacking people of color, 58
justice, 26, 61–62
    reproductive, 70, 108
    See also criminal justice system

King, Martin Luther, Jr., 89
kingdom of heaven, 92–101
kinship. *See* family

"Knowing More Than Is Good for One" (Mitzi Smith), 35

latchkey children, 91
Latinas. *See* Hispanic American women
Lawrence, Martin, 9
Leave It to Beaver (sitcom), 3
Lee, Jarena, 29–32, 36, 106
LGBTQ mothering, 109
liberation, 21, 26, 36
life
    essence of, 101
    quality of, 19, 26
Lil' Kim, 3, 79
Long, Nia, 79–80
love
    labor done out of, 23
    a mother's, 52–62
    of self, xii, 19
    of Spirit, 19, 21
low self-esteem, xv, 75, 81–82
Luke, Gospel of, 73–83

macrolinguistic studies, 34
Magnificat, 74, 76, 78
Making a Way Out of No Way (Coleman), 20–21
mammy, xiii, 3, 7–10, 15–16, 49–50
man's world, xv, 68, 71. *See also* patriarchy
marginalization, 44–45, 51, 78, 87–88, 90, 98
Mark, discipleship of, 34
Mark, Gospel of, 85
marriage, 5, 7, 11, 56, 76–77, 79–80, 91
    same-sex, 109
Martin, Clarice, 32–34, 36
Martin, Trayvon, 58
    Trayvon Martin Foundation, 52
Mary, various ones in the Bible, 73
Maryitis, 81–82
Mary Magdalene, 30, 73–74
Mary the mother of Jesus
    as favor(less) mother, xv, 73–83, 107
    overshadowing of, 77–78
    Virgin Mary theology, 74
materialism, xv
maternal instinct, 70

maternal obligations, 57, 91
maternal-rule traditions, 15
maternity leave, xiii
matriarchs/matriarchal structure, 4, 9–11, 13–16, 43–44, 64
matrifocal families, 11, 13, 15
matrilineality, 6–9, 15
Matthew, Gospel of, 84–101
    genealogy of Jesus, 86
    Great Commission of, 35
McBath, Lucia, 52, 61
McBride, Renisha, 58
McDonald, LaQuan, 53
McDonald's as firing for child endangerment, 17–18
McSpadden, Lesley, 52, 61
mediation, 89
mentors, 82–83, 107–8
Mephibosheth (Jonathan's son), 56
Mephibosheth (Rizpah's son), 56
Merab, 54–56, 58
Methodists, 14
middle class, 48, 84–85
Middle Passage, 5, 53
Miller-McLemore, Bonnie, 24
minimum wage workers, 18, 47, 91
ministry
    role of women in, 15
    See also calling; church mothers
Miriam (Song of), 78
Mississippi, 13
Missouri (Ferguson), 58
Mocha Moms network, xiii, 85
"mommy wars," 25
Moms Demand Action, 109
morality, drought in, 61–62
Moses, 29, 95
motherhood, 5
    as advocacy, xiv
    as process, 5
    the right to decide about, 70, 108
    role of mother, xvi
    See also African American mothers; *specific topics/descriptions*, e.g., matriarchs/matriarchal structure; single mothers/motherhood
Motherhood, Politics of (course), 108

mother of 2 Maccabees 7, 109
mother of James and John. *See* Zebedee's
  wife
mothers, current-day. *See* current-day
  mothers
mother scholars, xiii
mothers-in-law, 87, 109
mother-to-mother dependence, 11, 50–51
Mother Whore of Revelation, 109
Moynihan Report of 1965, 10
multidimensionality, 34
murder. *See* homicide
mythologies, 78

nameless mothers, 84
Nathan, 63–72
National Association for Children of
  Alcoholics, 61
National Association for the Advancement
  of Colored People (NAACP), 14
National Coalition for the Homeless,
  47–48
National Council of Negro Women, 14
Native Americans (percent of children
  born to single mothers), 79
Nazareth, 74–75, 79
Negro Family in the United States, The
  (Frazier), 41
New Testament, xii–xv, 32, 73
Northup, Solomon, 41
Nyong'o, Lupita, 41–42

Obama, Malia, 3
Obama, Michelle, 3
Obama, Sasha, 3
Old Testament, xii, xiv–xv, 32, 44, 66
one percent, the, 84
Onesimus, 33
oppression, 21, 34, 36
  dynamics between oppressed and
    oppressor, 50
  economic, 46
  oppressive structures, 26–27
  sexual, 46
  and systemic decay, 54
"other," women labeled as, xv
"other mothering," 9–15, 57
outsider language, 89–90

pain, a mother's, 52–62, 107
pastor/preacher mothers, xiii
patriarchy, xv, 14, 41–51, 63–91, 107
patrilineal structures/societies, 6, 54
Paul, St./epistles of, 28, 30–31
Pax Romana/"Peace of Rome," 77, 98
Pentateuch, four versions of (J, E, D, and
  P), 42n5
Perry, Tyler, 9
Peter, 95
  mother-in-law of, 109
Phoenicia, 86
Planned Parenthood, 70–71
plantation life, 7–8, 28
play mothers, xiii
politics
  freedom, political, 23, 26
  mothering in, xiii
  and not allowing societal/class status to
    limit abilities, 30–31
  political activism, 10, 30, 101
  political warfare, 58
  sociopolitical domination and
    exploitation, 76
  See also government
Politics of Motherhood course, 108
polygamy, 6
postbellum period, 49
postcolonial ideology, 34–35
poverty/the poor, 10, 15, 21, 48, 50, 58, 80
  child, 80
  the Lord as lifting the poor and
    marginalized, 78
  Song of Poor, 78
  the working poor, 18, 47, 91
power
  greatness as coming from service to
    humankind, 94, 101
  of Hagar, 44–45
  institutional, xv, 84–91
  of motherhood, 109
  powerlessness, 87
  those with power as needing to advocate
    for others on the margins, 14, 82
  women who engage institutional powers
    for the good of the children, xv, 84–91
  See also authority; *specific topics/*
    descriptions, e.g., Roman Empire

Pratt, Wanda, 100
praxis, xvi, 106
preachers/preaching
    pastor/preacher mothers, xiii
    a woman's call/right to, 30–31, 36
pregnancy
    of Mary, mother of Jesus, 73–83
    and the right to decide about
        motherhood, 70, 108
    teen, 12–13, 81
    unintended, 13, 60, 70
prejudice, class, 14
prestige, xv, 82, 98
priorities/prioritizing, 69–70
prison, 59–60
    African American men and, 59–60
    mothers with children in, xiv
    recidivism, 59–60
    school to prison pipeline, 107
    See also criminal justice system
Proctor, Samuel DeWitt, 88–89
proskyneo, 96–97
prostitution, 73, 89
Psalms, book of, 30

quality of life, 19, 26

Ra, the god, 45
race, xvi, 18–22, 26, 37, 46, 59, 87, 90
    dialogue among mothers of various
        racial and ethnic backgrounds, 109
    "other," women labeled as, xv
    racial identification, 22
    and womanist maternal thought,
        17–27
    See also intersection of race, gender,
        sexuality, and class
racism, 15, 17, 21–22, 27, 91, 106
    racial discrimination, 14
Rahab, 86
Raisin in the Sun, A (Hansberry), 11
rape, 7, 42, 46, 107
recidivism, 59–60
Reconstruction era, xiii, 4, 15, 24, 50, 57
relentlessness (of the Canaanite woman),
    xv, 84–91, 108, 110
"Religion and the Pure Principles of
    Morality" (Stewart), 30

reproductive justice, 70, 108
resurrection of Jesus, 96
Revelation, book of, 32, 34, 109
Rhimes, Shonda, 3
rich, the, 78, 84, 98
righteousness, drought in, 61–62
Rizpah, xiv, 107
    as childless mother, 52–62
Roman Empire, 73–83, 92–101
    Pax Romana, 77, 98

sacrifice, 57, 88, 101
salvation/salvation history, 86, 107
same-sex marriage, 109
Samuel, books of, 52–62, 64–66, 78
Sarah/Sarai, 41–51
Saul, King, 52–62
scandal, 63
Schneider, Tammi J., 44–45
school
    after-school networks, 91
    discipline, harshness of, 59
    homeless shelters, children who go to
        school from, 48
    mothers as principle teachers and
        nurturers, 4
    school to prison pipeline, 107
    suspensions, 59
    time children spend at, 4
    and training at home, 4
    See also education
Scott, Stuart, 94
Scripture. *See* Bible
2 Maccabees 7, mother of, 109
segregation, 80
servants/servanthood, 8–9, 44–46, 75
    greatness as coming from service to
        humankind, 94, 101
sexism, 14–15, 18, 21–22, 27, 55, 77, 88,
    91, 106
sexual dynamics
    after the Emancipation Proclamation, 50
    "mammy" as asexualized, 7–9
    relations between men in power and
        slave women, 41–51, 57, 107
    See also intersection of race, gender,
        sexuality, and class; *individual names,*
        e.g., Bathsheba

sexual intercourse
  Mary, mother of Jesus and, 73–83
  teens as postponing, 12
sexual oppression, 46
Shakur, Afeni, 52
Shakur, Tupac, 52
sharing, 98
shelters. *See under* homelessness: homeless
  shelters
Shepherd, Sherri, 49
Sherman, Bracey, 60
shiphchah, 44–45
sick days, 47
*Simon of Cyrene: A Case of Roman
  Conscription* (Crowder), 34n24
single fathers, 4
single mothers/motherhood, xi, 10, 88
  financial challenges for, 80–81
  Hagar as, 41–51
  Mary as, 73–83
  per cent of children born to, 79
  racial backdrop of, 79–80
single parents, 4, 48, 58, 81
sister bonds among mothers, 15
"sistermotherly" regard, 27
slavery, xiii, 3–10, 28–29, 53
  enslavement, 7–9, 23–24, 107
  Hagar as slave, xiv, 41–51, 107
  language of, 75
  mammy, xiii, 3, 7–10, 15–16, 49–50
  relations between men in power and
    slave women, 41–51, 57, 107
  structures of, 15
  Twelve Years a Slave (movie), 41–42
Smiley, Rickey, 9
Smith, Amanda Berry, 29
Smith, Mitzi, 32, 35
Smith, Shanell, 32–34
Smith, Susan, 110
social class. *See* class
social death, 59
social mobility, xv, 98
Society of Biblical Literature (SBL),
  xii–xiii
socio-economic status. *See under* class
Solomon, xv, 63–72

Southeastern Conference on the Study of
  Religion (SECSOR), xiv
Spirit, love for, 19, 20
sports, 92–101
sports mothers, 99–101
status. *See* class
stay-at-home dads, 4
stay-at-home mothers, xiii, 3, 23–25, 70,
  89–90
St. Clair, Rachel, 21, 32–34, 36
stereotypes, 11, 19, 60
Stewart, Maria W., 20, 29–32, 36
stigma, social, xv, 10, 79, 107
strength, xvii, 11, 15, 18–19, 63, 70, 110
subordination, 87
success (pressure for children to succeed/
  mother's lack of success), xv, 92–101
Sudarkasa, Niara, 6
surrogacy, xiv, 50
  of Hagar, xiv, 41–51, 107
survival, xii–xiii, xv, 6–7, 10, 18–19, 24,
  26, 46, 51, 58–59, 79, 85
Syrophoenician mother, 85
systemic decay, 54

Tamar, 86
teaching/teachers
  the Great Commission to, 35
  mothers as, 4
teen mothers, xiii
  family structure and, 12–13
  Mary the mother of Jesus as, xv, 73–83,
    107
  stigmas surrounding, xv, 107
  teen birth rates/teen pregnancy rate,
    12, 81
Terrell, Mary Church, 14, 24, 27, 82
theology/theologies, xiv
  African American community's
    experience in the context of, xiv
  African American women in, 21
  feminist, 20–21
  sexist, 14
  womanist, 19–20
theophanies, 46
Thurman, Howard, 28

"tiger mom," 109
*Too Heavy a Yoke: Black Women and the
    Burden of Strength* (Walker-Barnes),
    18–19
training in the home, 4
Transfiguration, 95
Trayvon Martin Foundation, 52
Truth, Sojourner, 29
Tubman, Harriet, 28–29
Twelve Years a Slave (movie), 41–42
two-parent households, 4, 84

"Ubuntu," 27, 82
unemployment, 80, 84
United States, 61–62
    feminist movement in, 20
    relevance of womanist maternal
        thinking for African American
        mothers in, xiv
    See also specific topics, e.g., slavery
Uriah, 64

values
    and drought in morality, 61–62
    instilling children with, 4, 22n13, 85
    spiritual, 22n13
violence, xiv, 46, 52
    domestic, 60–61
    gun, 52–53, 109
    mothers who have lost children to, xiv,
        52–62
    See also homicide
virginity, 73–83
Virgin Mary theology, 74
vision mothers, 13–16
vocation, xii, 26. *See also* calling
voting, 13, 60

wages/income
    and African-American men, 10
    exploitative, 23
    and the middle class, 48
    See also minimum wage workers
Walker, Alice, xii, 19–21, 32, 35–36
Walker-Barnes, Chanequa, 18–19
Wall Street, 68–69

war, 87, 98
    mothers who have lost children to, xiv
Waters, John, 44
Wattleton, Faye, 70–72
"weaker" versus "stronger" ideology, 77
Weems, Renita, 22, 32–33, 36
welfare, 10, 61, 79–80, 89–91
Wells, Ida B., 20, 24, 27, 29, 82
West African tribes/cultures, 5–7, 15
wet nursing, 107
whore of Babylon, 34
Wilkerson, Ebony, 109
Williams, Delores S., 19, 45–46, 50
Williams, Serena, 99
Williams, Venus, 99
Wisdom, book of, 105
womanism, xiv, 18–21
    feminism and, 19–21, 33–35
womanist biblical hermeneutics/
        interpretation, xiv, 19, 21, 28–37,
        106–7
womanist maternal thought, xiii–xiv,
        17–27, 109
work, 89
    advocacy as, 27, 89, 91
    for African American women/mothers,
        23–27, 68–71
    African American women-owned
        businesses, 68
    domestic, 8, 57
    in a man's corporate world, xv, 63–72
    paid and unpaid, 84–91
    professional and managerial positions,
        xiii, 9, 48
    triple consciousness of family, work,
        and community, 24, 82
    See also career; *topics beginning with
        "job"; specific topics/descriptions,* e.g.,
        entrepreneurship; minimum wage
        workers
working mothers, 18, 23–26, 85, 89–90
    as breadwinners, 4, 10
worship, 34, 47, 77

Zebedee's wife, xv, 88
    as shameless mother, 92–101

CPSIA information can be obtained
at www.ICGtesting.com
Printed in the USA
FFOW02n2105230517
35957FF